Baby to Toddler
Month by Month

Baby to Toddler

Month by Month

Follows Your Baby's Journey from 6 to 23 Months

Simone Cave and
Dr Caroline Fertleman

HAY HOUSE

Carlsbad, California • New York City
London • Sydney • New Delhi

Published in the United Kingdom by:
Hay House UK Ltd, The Sixth Floor, Watson House,
54 Baker Street, London W1U 7BU
Tel: +44 (0)20 3927 7290; Fax: +44 (0)20 3927 7291; www.hayhouse.co.uk

Published in the United States of America by:
Hay House Inc., PO Box 5100, Carlsbad, CA 92018-5100
Tel: (1) 760 431 7695 or (800) 654 5126
Fax: (1) 760 431 6948 or (800) 650 5115; www.hayhouse.com

Published in Australia by:
Hay House Australia Ltd, 18/36 Ralph St, Alexandria NSW 2015
Tel: (61) 2 9669 4299; Fax: (61) 2 9669 4144; www.hayhouse.com.au

Published in India by:
Hay House Publishers India, Muskaan Complex, Plot No.3, B-2,
Vasant Kunj, New Delhi 110 070
Tel: (91) 11 4176 1620; Fax: (91) 11 4176 1630; www.hayhouse.co.in

A catalogue record for this book is available from the British Library.

ISBN 978-1-84850-209-3

Printed and bound by CPI Group (UK) Ltd, Croydon, CR0 4YY

To Lewis, Douglas, Natalie, Harry, Tobias and Betsy

CONTENTS

Contents

ACKNOWLEDGEMENTS

We would like to thank Paul Johnson, Judy Cave and Barbara Levy. And also numerous healthcare professionals at The Whittington Hospital and elsewhere for their invaluable input. Those we would particularly like to thank are Sam Behjati, Mike Cave, Sheila Doherty, Adam Fox, Linda Greenwall, Deborah Hodes, Kate Hodge and Susan Leigh.

And finally, we'd like to thank the following babies and toddlers who, unknowingly, have been a huge help with our observational research: Natalie, Martha, Gabby, Maisy, Lena, Marie Josephine, Sebastian, David, Eva, Ethan, Esme and Charlie.

INTRODUCTION

The early years of parenthood are a magical time, and you will already have watched your tiny newborn grow into a big chuckling baby who flirts with the world. Well, the show doesn't stop here – and some would say the fun is really about to begin. You have front-row seats to one of the most entertaining and often hilarious stages of childhood – when your baby grows into a toddler.

Over the next 18 months you will witness your 6-month-old baby transform into a running, talkative toddler with attitude.

Following the success of our first book, *Your Baby Week by Week*, which takes you from birth to 6 months, we have been inundated with requests for a follow-up book. And now it's here – *Baby to Toddler Month by Month* follows the journey from month 6 to month 23 – just at the point when your baby is about to turn 2.

You've no doubt become highly competent at looking after your baby over the last 6 months, but now you will need a whole new set of skills as you help your little one with her first mouthfuls of solid food, her first steps and her first words. You'll also need a few tricks up your sleeve to cope when your toddler throws her lunch across the kitchen or flatly refuses to go in her buggy. She will quite literally throw her toys out of her pram.

We haven't given you magic answers in this book because, despite having had six toddlers between us, we simply haven't found any. Of course we've shared our favourite tips and tricks, which we know work. But more important than giving you solutions, we have focused on giving perspective and understanding. You can't change the nature of toddlers – and thank goodness. But if you understand a little of what's going on in their minds, it can give you a window into their world and a degree of patience with whatever they're getting up to.

For example, when your 15-month-old suddenly starts making a big fuss at bedtime and hates you leaving the room, it is most likely because separation anxiety peaks at this age and she is genuinely anxious. With this in mind, we suggest a way of resolving the problem. And when your 22-month-old toddler shrieks, 'mine' and refuses to share a toy kettle with another child, it's comforting to know that this is a normal developmental stage that happens once your child is able to see herself as a separate and independent person.

Having this month-by-month insight into your child's developmental changes will make her behaviour seem fascinating rather than alarming and overwhelming.

We've referred to your child as 'she' in this book, simply because in our last book we opted for 'he', and it seems only fair. And because there's no clearly defined moment when a baby turns into a toddler, we use the term 'baby' from months 6 to 12, after which we use both 'baby' and 'toddler'. Then as we approach month 23 we gradually reduce the number of references to 'baby' and increase the use of 'toddler' until we're using 'toddler' exclusively. This seems to match how parents refer to their own children at these ages.

Throughout the book we have tried to avoid giving strict instructions on how to bring up your child, because this is a very individual thing and, anyway, children don't conform to textbooks. As with our last book we have adopted a gentler, more advisory approach, giving you information and, hopefully, an understanding of the changes your child is going through so that you can make informed decisions and feel confident that you are doing the best you can for your child.

WEANING

This is a huge subject and something that parents often worry about. There's more confusion than ever at the moment because UK Government guidelines have changed, and also it's become fashionable to follow baby-led weaning.

We have given you the very latest information (at the time of going to print) and enough background facts on the various weaning methods so that you can make your own informed decision on how to wean your baby.

We also have an entire chapter on planning meals for your baby, which covers finger foods, purees and how to include your baby in family meals from day one.

And of course we cover healthy diet as well as how to deal with the various challenges you may face over the coming months, such as fussy eating or refusing to eat at all.

There's so much pressure on parents to feed their toddlers healthily that this can be a very stressful time. But with our month-by-month guidance you will hopefully avoid many of the thorny issues altogether. It's quite common, for example, for babies to refuse to eat lumpy food. But if you know this in advance and also know what to do, you can avoid it ever becoming a problem.

GETTING THE MOST FROM *BABY TO TODDLER*

Having a child aged between 6 and 24 months will mean that you are very busy, so we have made it easy for you to find what you are looking for. Read the month that is appropriate to your baby's age – beginning at 6 months. Then follow each month after that until your child's second birthday.

You don't have to read the entire chapter – simply pick out the headings that are relevant to you – for example Sleep, or perhaps Feeding. And if you can't find what you are looking for, then you can skip ahead a month or two. Your baby will never be an exact match to the book because all babies are different and develop at different rates. You can also, of course, use the book's Index to help find answers to specific questions.

Milestones

Every month we have included a 'Milestones' section where we have listed various developmental goals that your baby may reach – though please don't worry if she doesn't reach them all bang on schedule! All babies are different, so each parent will tick off different milestones. The idea isn't to get as many ticks as possible – it's not a competition. You probably wouldn't notice half of these milestones if you weren't looking out for them. The aim of this section is really just to have a bit of fun and to engage more with your baby. You may go back and tick off some of the milestones a month or so later, and some you may never tick at all.

Within this section you may often find yourself skipping back or ahead a few months – if your baby is a quick walker but a slow talker, for instance, you will always be reading a few months behind when it comes to talking. That's fine – read the book in the way that works best for you and your child.

When to Worry

Of course it's easy to worry about your baby and wonder if she is normal and progressing at a normal pace, so we have also included 'When to Worry' boxes so that you can quickly see if she may be falling behind or if she has some other issue that is holding her back, such as, for example, a hearing problem.

The aim of these boxes is first to help the majority of parents relax and enjoy their babies, safe in the knowledge that they have nothing to worry about. Secondly it is to help the small minority of parents to spot the early warning signs that doctors will pick up on. Medical and developmental problems are easier to treat if they are picked up early, for example if a hearing problem is discovered early it will minimize any impact on speech development.

When to See the Doctor

This section of each month includes information on common ailments. We have tried to predict roughly in which months they are likely to occur, but this is far from an exact science. Having said that, the information will still obviously be useful even if your baby suffers from, say, constipation in a different month to the one we included it under.

As we stress in the book, always seek medical advice if you are in any way concerned about your child. Your GP will be happy to see you and your child, even if it's only to offer reassurance that your toddler is fit and well.

Safety Tip of the Month

Each month includes one of these tips, and again we have tried to anticipate which month each tip will be most relevant. Again, though, each baby is unique, so some of our tips will be in the 'wrong' month. If your child is particularly advanced at walking, for instance, it may be an idea to read the safety tips for a few months ahead.

WHO IS THE BOOK FOR?

As parents, we wish we'd had such a book when our children were under 2. Anything to have increased our patience levels and helped us cope with the frustrations would have been incredibly welcome.

Of course first-time parents will benefit – both mums and dads. But we also recommend this book for those with more than one child – particularly for the weaning section. Feeding advice will almost certainly have changed since you weaned your older children, and you will probably find that weaning is easier these days because there are fewer worries about allergies and fewer restrictions on what your baby can eat.

We hope that having *Baby to Toddler Month by Month* to hand will help with the practical problems as you cope with some of the confusion and frustrations of bringing up small children. But also we want to bring a sense of perspective so that you can enjoy the fun and, frankly, sheer hilarity of life with toddlers who, by their very nature, are irresistibly lovable even when they're at their very worst.

Enjoy!

MONTH 6

INTRODUCTION

Now that your baby is 6 months old, you probably feel that life is a little more under control than when she was a tiny baby. You know roughly how each day is going to pan out because your baby will be in some sort of feeding and sleeping routine. Simple things like having to pop out to the shops or catch a bus or train with your baby in tow no longer seem like major operations that send you into a mini-panic.

Well, things are about to kick off again – in the next few months your baby is going to start moving – which will certainly keep you busy as you'll have to watch her constantly to check that she comes to no harm.

The biggest change in month 6, though, is that she will start to eat solids. Watching your baby cross this huge milestone and take her first few mouthfuls of real food is very special. She's leaving behind the days of being a milk-dependent infant, and she will soon be tucking into family meals and enjoying whatever you're eating.

Some parents introduce their babies to solids at 4 months, as we explained in our last book, *Your Baby Week by Week*. But if you have waited until now to wean your baby, you can take a much more relaxed approach and perhaps even try *baby-led weaning*: when babies are weaned straight onto finger food and skip the puree stage. Or you can try a combination of purees and finger foods – again, this is a very relaxed approach and your baby will be able to join in with family meals from day one. We give you all the facts on weaning to help you choose the method that will suit your baby, and you, best.

But moving on to solids isn't the only milestone this month, because at around this time, lots of babies start to roll across the room, or even creep along on their tummies. And plenty of babies will learn to sit this month, too. Unlike walking and talking, you don't hear people making a big fuss when a baby learns to sit up on her own. But being able to sit is a big developmental step, as it means she'll soon be able to sit in a highchair, and also sit up and play with toys.

SLEEP

Each month we will suggest the ideal sleeping pattern for a baby of this age, but do be aware that plenty of babies won't follow it, or may not follow it consistently.

Aim: *uninterrupted night sleep 8–12 hours*
To bed early – about 7 or 8 p.m.
Two naps: *short (30- to 40-minutes) morning nap, longer lunchtime nap (2–3 hours)*
A total of 14½ hours' sleep

Naps

Your baby may have several short naps throughout the day whenever she gets the opportunity – perhaps in her buggy, in the car or in your arms after a feed. The advantage of a relaxed napping pattern is that you don't have to plan your day around your baby's naps. The downside is that your baby may not yet be having a long lunchtime nap, which would give you a 2-hour break.

If you want, you can steer your baby towards this by putting her in her cot at around the same time after lunch and gradually teaching her that this is nap time. Or you can keep to your own less structured napping pattern if that suits you better. And lots of mums let their baby have a longer morning nap and then go out to meet other mums and babies for lunch. With naps, there's plenty of flexibility.

Night-time

You may not want to take quite such a laissez-faire approach to night sleeping habits. If your baby still isn't yet sleeping through the night, you'll probably be completely exhausted. But take comfort in the fact that you're far from alone, because even at 9 months at least 30 per cent of babies still aren't sleeping through, according to the National Sleep Foundation. And there's plenty you can do, as we'll explain next month.

Her Own Room

You may well be moving your baby to her own room around now, because at 6 months the risk of cot death is vastly reduced and you no longer need to take the precaution of sleeping in the same room as your baby (room-sharing is known to cut the risk of cot death).

To prepare your baby for her new room you can both spend some time playing in it in the days leading up to her move. You could also give your baby her bedtime milk feed in her new room before returning her to sleep in her cot in your room. It may take a couple of nights for your baby to adapt to her new room, but at 6 months she will still be pretty flexible and should get used to it quickly.

If while sharing a room you were sensitive to her every cry and snuffle, then you'll really benefit from no longer being woken by her minor night awakenings – you'll only have to get up for the bigger problems. This in turn will teach your baby to become better at settling herself back to sleep because you're not attending to her every cry.

The big disadvantage of no longer sharing a room is that when your baby does cry, it's more effort for you to have to go into another room to settle her.

You may want to wait until your baby has grown out of night-feeds before you move her into her own room (see below).

Dropping the Night-feed

Many babies will have dropped their night-feed by now, but if your baby still wants hers, then this will be due to either habit or hunger.

- Hunger – the biggest giveaway is that she used to sleep through the night and has suddenly started waking again, either during the night or very early in the morning. Once your baby starts solids, this should resolve itself.
- Habit – the clue here is that your baby wakes at the same time each night. This is more difficult to resolve. Start by ensuring that she's having plenty of milk during the day (four or five feeds) and try to get her to drink a big milk feed at bedtime. Then give her a little less milk during each night-feed until she's no longer waking (if you're breastfeeding, feed for less time). This sounds so simple, but the reality is that it will take effort and determination on your part because your baby will take longer to settle after her somewhat reduced feed. Sadly there's no shortcut solution, you just have to grit your teeth and get on with it and accept you're going to be even more exhausted than usual for a while. But you will hopefully be rewarded by waking up one morning and realizing your baby slept through the night. As a very last resort, you could always try controlled crying (see Month 7).

Troubleshooting

She falls asleep late afternoon, then won't settle at bedtime

Your baby probably dropped her late afternoon nap (third nap of the day) when she was around 5 months old. You may find that if you're out in the car, or your baby is in her buggy at around this time, she still drops off late in the afternoon, especially if she's had a busy day. The one advantage of this is that it will make her less cranky for the final stretch of the day. But the disadvantage is you may find her more difficult to settle at bedtime, so you can try and plan your day so that she doesn't get the opportunity for this late afternoon nap, as most babies this age no longer need it. But if this isn't possible, just put her to bed a little later.

FEEDING

Aim: *By the end of the month your baby may be eating three small meals a day, including some iron-rich foods such as meat. She will hopefully be playing with finger food and perhaps eating some. And she will probably be having four to six milk feeds. She may drop a milk feed or two during the month.*

Meal Planning

We have written a chapter on planning meals for your baby which includes lots of ideas for preparing purees, lumpy purees, mashes, finger foods, iron-rich foods, vegetarian foods and meals you can share with your baby. You can read this chapter (see page 237) in conjunction with the weaning information we give each month.

If your baby hasn't tried solids yet, then it's time to begin – don't delay weaning, because your baby needs the iron and also needs to learn to chew.

The Department of Health recommends waiting until 6 months to begin weaning onto solids. By this age, your baby will be able to eat most foods and so join in with family meals, and will also be old enough to try finger foods. We think that 6 months is the best age to wean because it is easier than doing it earlier, and also babies get maximum benefit from breastfeeding.

Having said this, please don't worry if your baby is already on solids – plenty of mums begin from around 4 months, and the latest scientific opinion from the European Food Safety Authority (EFSA) states that it is safe to begin solids whilst still breastfeeding, at any time between 4 and 6 months. And solids shouldn't be delayed after 6 months, as this may affect growth.

If your baby has yet to start on solids, then you need to decide how to begin. Here are three methods – our favourite is 'combination weaning', a mix of introducing purees and finger foods which ensures your baby moves from milk to solids swiftly and has all the nutrients she needs. We also like baby-led weaning, although this won't suit everyone. But we don't recommend the traditional puree method for babies over 6 months, as this is the method most likely to lead to feeding problems later on.

1. The Traditional Puree Method

Back in the 1960s, babies started solids at 3 months or younger. Then the guidelines moved the recommended age to 4 months, and now it's 6.

The Method
You give your baby fine purees of single fruits and vegetables or baby rice, and after several months gradually advance to lumpy food and then finger food.

The Problems
This method may be fine for a 4-month-old baby, but at 6 months a baby needs to progress onto more grown-up food quickly so that she has enough

iron, and also gets used to eating lumpy foods and learns to chew. Many babies get stuck on purees for too long and find it difficult to progress.

If you want to give your baby purees, it's important to progress quickly onto thicker, lumpier and mashed foods, and include lots of iron-rich foods such as meat in her diet. We explain how to do this in our halfway house method, Combination Weaning (see page 9).

2. Baby-led Weaning

This is when babies always feed themselves, and the method has become very fashionable in the last few years. We like it because it takes a very relaxed approach to eating, and babies are never encouraged or forced to eat against their will.

Advocates would argue that baby-led weaning is very natural because self-feeding supports a baby's motor development – just as she is learning to grasp, she will be given tempting food to play with and taste, and this will help develop her new grasping skills. Also, babies learn to chew at around the time they learn to grasp – usually between 6 and 8 months.

To do baby-led weaning, your baby should be 6 months old, able to sit up, and have good neck control.

The Method

Your baby feeds herself with finger foods from her very first meal (for example some broccoli, pasta pieces and some sliced, hard-boiled egg, or soft-cooked chicken to suck).

In baby-led weaning you don't help your baby to eat – even if she's eating yoghurt or porridge, you give her a spoon and let her copy you. The idea is that you never spoon food into your baby's mouth – she feeds herself and decides what and when she wants to eat. And you mustn't be tempted to fill your baby up afterwards by spooning in puree. The theory is that she gets all her nourishment from milk as she plays with the food initially, then as she gradually starts to eat she is able to drop some of her milk feeds – perhaps after a couple of months or so. So when you start, you offer your baby solids *after* her milk feed.

The Problems

Meals are time-consuming and messy, which some mums find stressful. And it's more difficult to monitor how much your baby has eaten – you have to trust that your baby has had enough, which can be worrying for some people.

Baby-led weaning is quite a rigid method in that it discourages you from spoon-feeding your baby, and initially you are supposed to offer your baby food *after* her milk feed – but some babies get quite sleepy after a milk feed.

Although some babies take quickly to baby-led weaning and never have a single spoonful of puree, others aren't ready to eat finger foods at 6 months and remain dependent on breastmilk or formula. This is OK for a month or two, but do bear in mind that iron stores start to run low in breastfed babies at 6 months.

Another reason that baby-led weaning can result in a baby having too little iron is if you don't give your baby enough iron-rich finger foods. Not everyone has the time to carefully plan and prepare nutritious meals, and the temptation can be to let your baby suck on a custard cream or other convenience food.

If your baby was born premature, you will need to speak to your doctor because your baby may not learn to chew until later than 6 months. And babies with special needs who have problems with fine motor skills and chewing may not be able to pick up the food competently enough, nor chew it.

3. Combination Weaning – Purees and Finger Foods

Giving your baby a combination of purees and finger foods is our favourite weaning method. Your baby will quickly get much of her nutrition from the purees, as they start to replace milk feeds, and at the same time she will have fun playing with finger foods.

Our 'halfway house' method is based on the Department of Health's guidelines – these say you should begin the weaning process with purees and mashed foods at 6 months, and also include finger foods as soon as your baby is ready. Some babies seem ready at 6 months, others wait until they are 7 or 8 months old before starting finger foods.

Interestingly, the DoH has updated its advice on how to wean since the recommended weaning age went up to 6 months in 2003: the key message these days is that weaning babies is a lot more relaxed than it used to be because they are older when they start.

We like the baby-led weaning approach, but we also think a little gentle help spooning puree to your baby in the early days certainly isn't harmful. Feeding your baby with a spoon and helping her to eat is very natural. Humans have been giving their babies mashed-up food since time began. And around the world, mothers help their babies to eat.

> Please be aware that it's important not to put solid lumps of food into your baby's mouth because it may be a choking risk. She has to pick finger food up herself – see Safety Tip of the Month, page 19.

The Method

You give your baby purees and also finger foods right from the start, as long as she is able to sit well. The basic rule is, if she can sit in a highchair, she can eat finger foods – a few babies will have to wait until next month.

Offer your baby solids when she is a little hungry – about 30 minutes before her milk feed is due. If she's too hungry she'll get upset because she will only be able to eat slowly in the early stages. Milk is still providing most of her nutrition.

From day one of weaning she can sit down for family lunch with a bowl of puree that you spoon to her, and then she can help herself to anything from the table – perhaps a well-cooked bit of carrot, potato or a slice of meat to suck.

You can offer your baby pretty much any food from the start and let her try what you are eating as long as it's not off-limits (see 'Foods to Avoid' page 14). And you don't have to worry about allergies (see Month 7 section, 'Allergies', page 32).

Do stick to healthy foods, and include lots of different vegetables and fruit because you're setting up the foundations for a healthy diet.

Allow your baby to set the pace – playing with finger foods and deciding how much puree she wants. The idea is that you stop feeding her puree as soon as she's had enough, not for you to try to 'get the last bit down her'.

You can offer pieces of finger food with each meal and let your baby decide if she wants to play with them or indeed eat them. Then, as she becomes more interested in finger foods over the coming weeks, you can increase the finger foods and decrease the purees. Likewise, you can reduce her milk feeds as she becomes more dependent on solids. So be brave, give your baby lots of finger foods, and don't get stuck on pureed carrots for too long.

The Problems

Some babies absolutely refuse to eat from a spoon, in which case baby-led weaning would be a better option.

Drinks

Give your baby water to drink from a free-flowing beaker – non-spill beakers continue to promote sucking, not drinking, which means that your baby sucks a little bit of liquid straight to the back of her mouth instead of having large amounts of liquid in her mouth. The sooner your baby makes this transition, the better. She can also try an open cup with supervision.

You can offer your baby drinks both with her meal and in between. And if you are drinking water yourself, let her share. Babies don't always like water to begin with, but persevere. Don't be tempted by juices and squashes because they cause tooth decay, even when diluted.

You can also start giving your baby milk out of a cup instead of a bottle around now. This works well for her breakfast milk, but you may find that for her nap-time and bedtime milk she still wants a bottle if she finds it comforting. Don't leave your baby to sleep with a bottle, as this will cause tooth decay.

How to Begin – Baby Rice and Finger Food

You can start with baby rice which, although old-fashioned, makes a great first meal. You can also give your baby some finger food to play with – just an experiment at this stage, to see what she does.

> See our Meal Planning chapter for making purees, lumpy purees, mashes, finger foods, iron-rich foods, vegetarian foods, and meals you can share with your baby.

Baby Rice

Boxed, dried rice from supermarkets and chemists is what 4-month-old babies were weaned on in days gone by, but even today there are advantages to using old-fashioned baby rice for your baby's first few meals. Because you mix it up with breastmilk or formula, it will taste bland and familiar so your baby won't have to cope with new flavours at the same time as having solids in her mouth. Also, the consistency is like thick soup to begin with, which makes swallowing easy. And, best of all, baby rice is fortified with iron.

Your baby will probably be quite surprised to have solids in her mouth and may spit them out at first. But keep spooning gently and don't worry if she eats very little. Your goal is to introduce her to the experience of having solid food in her mouth, not to give her a big meal. She'll gradually learn how to move the food from the front to the back of her mouth and, as she does this, she'll start to swallow – this sometimes takes a few days.

You can use a specially designed baby spoon, available from supermarkets and chemists – these are made of soft plastic so are less likely to hurt the gums than metal.

> Once your baby is 6 months you can begin weaning with any puree – just mix it up with breastmilk or formula so that it is runny and easy for your baby's first meal.

Finger Foods

Begin with something easy to hold and swallow, such as a piece of broccoli or a slice of toast (toast is better than bread, which can stick to the roof of the mouth).

Once your baby has had some baby rice, put the finger food in front of her and see if she picks it up. She may not be interested; perhaps she'll pick it up and put it to her mouth but not really eat anything. Or she may even eat a little. It doesn't actually matter at this stage, because it's just fun.

What Next?

If your baby seems quite surprised and doesn't eat much the first time you give her solids, continue to offer her plain baby rice a few more times until she gets the hang of eating it.

As for finger foods, continue to give your baby bits of food to play with. She'll enjoy the colours and textures even if she doesn't eat. And you can always eat it yourself once she's had a play, to show her what to do.

Once your baby seems to be getting the hang of her rice (often after a day or two babies will eat a very small bowlful), you can start thinking about balanced meals and different ways of including enough iron in your baby's diet. You also need to think about consistency, so that your baby learns to chew (babies can chew with their gums even before they have any teeth).

Giving Your Baby Enough Iron

A baby's iron stores are depleted by about 6 months, and her iron requirements increase at around this time, too. If babies aren't given sufficient iron-rich foods such as meat and eggs, they can become anaemic. One of the symptoms of anaemia is appetite loss, which perpetuates the problem – this is one of the reasons older babies can end up in a paediatric feeding clinic. (See our Meal Planning chapter for more on iron-rich foods.)

Thickening Up Purees

Purees don't teach babies to chew, so you need to thicken them up to prepare your baby for lumps (more on lumps next month!).

Add baby rice to purees to gradually thicken the consistency over the next few days until it doesn't fall off the spoon when you tip it.

How Much to Feed Your Baby

Your baby will probably eat anything from a couple of teaspoons to a small bowl of food at each meal – it will almost certainly vary from day to day.

You can increase your baby's solids to twice a day some time during the first fortnight. At this stage it doesn't matter if she seems to be eating very little – it's more about experimenting with textures and flavours. You'll find that sometimes she hardly eats anything, and at other times she may eat a lot. If you are offering your baby solid food twice a day, you can let her take the lead in how much she eats. And always keep mealtimes fun and relaxed.

In the second half of the month you can increase your baby's meals to three a day if she seems to be eating a little at each sitting and enjoying her food. Follow your baby's lead, but try to ensure that she's having three meals a day by the time she is 9 months old.

What Time to Feed Your Baby

You can feed your baby at around the time she has her milk feeds to coincide with breakfast, lunch and tea. She will probably end up having her breakfast at about 7 a.m. – this can be a bit later if you give her an early morning milk feed. Then lunch at about 11.30 a.m. – 12 midday. And finally, tea at around 5 p.m. Plus a couple of snacks between meals if your baby gets hungry.

All families follow different timetables, but because most toddlers and babies go to bed early, their mealtimes tend to follow quite an early pattern as well.

Babies and young children need to eat regularly, and don't cope well if they are hungry – most become tearful and bad-tempered – which is why parents usually stick to quite rigid feeding schedules.

It's also helpful to get your baby into a feeding routine, because if she is fed at around the same time each day she'll become hungry at these times.

We found it helpful to give our babies a big milk feed after lunch, as this helps settle them for their afternoon nap. But there's no right or wrong way.

Foods to Avoid

- Whole nuts, grapes, cherries or cherry tomatoes, which your baby could choke on. Peanut butter or nut paste is OK (unless there is a family history of nut allergy). And you can chop the other foods in half and remove stones from cherries. Children shouldn't have 'choking' foods until they are 5.

- Biscuits and sugary foods – the longer you can keep your baby off sweet foods, the better, because sugar will give your baby a sweet tooth.
- Honey – honey very occasionally contains bacteria which cause infant botulism in babies under 1 year old.
- Low-fat milk and yoghurt – babies need full-fat dairy products until they are 2, because the fat helps with brain development and also helps vitamin absorption.
- Salt – babies' kidneys are too immature to cope with a diet high in salt, and for long-term health we should all be eating less salt to reduce the risk of stroke and heart disease. So avoid salty foods such as sausages and packet-foods not aimed at babies, and don't add salt to your baby's food in her first year. This also includes soy sauce, stock cubes and gravies, which are very high in salt. If your baby occasionally grabs at something containing salt that the rest of the family are eating (say, pizza or Chinese noodles) then don't worry too much – just try to keep her overall salt intake to a minimum.
- High-fibre foods – wholemeal pasta, wholemeal bread, brown rice, pulses and lentils are all full of fibre, which is bulky and fills babies up without giving them many calories. While these foods are healthy options for adults, babies should only eat wholemeal foods every few days to get them used to the taste. And once they are eating three meals a day, they should have no more than one wholemeal food a day.

DEVELOPMENT AND PLAY

Talking

Your baby will enjoy the sound of her own voice and sometimes will babble away saying consonants such as ba-ba, ga-ga, da-da and ma-ma.

You'll notice that your baby sometimes does a 'fake' angry-sounding cry to get your attention – for example she wants to get down from the highchair or out of her buggy. Although she doesn't yet have any words, she is able to make herself clearly understood – listen out for her 'demand' cry and try to work out what she wants. She'll be delighted when you get it right and will stop crying instantly.

MILESTONES

(All babies are different – you probably won't be able to tick everything on this list.)

☐ *Rolling* – babies learn to roll from their fronts to their backs from as early as 4 months. And around now, many of them learn to roll from their backs onto their tummies, which means they can roll all the way over and move across the room. Be careful – lots of parents get caught out and are amazed to discover their babies on the other side of the room. So check for anything dangerous such as large vases, or small objects she can put in her mouth. Your baby will need to be watched most of the time once she is on the move, and of course you should never leave her on a bed, changing table or sofa unattended, in case she rolls off. Some babies skip the rolling stage and go straight from sitting to crawling. This is probably because they have had minimal tummy time so haven't built up their muscles sufficiently to roll. But it's nothing to worry about – they all seem to catch up in the end.

☐ *Sitting* – your baby may be able to sit by herself for about 10 seconds before toppling over – her head is still big for her body, making her wobble. She'll support herself by putting her hands on the floor, but do make sure she is on a soft surface and there's nothing hard that she might fall against. As she develops strength in her hips and spine this month she may be able to sit for longer – you can prop her up with cushions. At first she'll put a hand on the floor for balance, then after a few weeks she'll stop needing this extra support and be able to sit and play with toys. Don't let your baby sit for too long at first, because she'll become tired and her head will fall back and she'll fall over. She should still be spending lots of time playing on her tummy.

☐ *Ready for a highchair* – some babies will be ready this month, but lots will only be able to sit for a couple of minutes. You can put your baby on your knee for meals.

☐ *Creeping* – if your baby is going to be an early crawler she will be creeping by now, shunting herself along on her tummy. Crawling usually starts 2 months after creeping. Encourage her by putting a toy in front of her to see if she tries to shunt towards it – some babies will try then give up and wait a couple of weeks until the whole exercise gets a bit easier. Others will be determined to get to the toy and can end up in a frustrated rage as they struggle. It's fascinating to see personality emerging at such a young age.

☐ *Object permanence* – at around 6 months babies develop 'object permanence'. Before this they think that if they can't see something then it doesn't exist. Now they are old enough to play peek-a-boo – if you hide behind a door or your hands and then emerge saying 'boo', your baby will be delighted. She'll know you're still there and are about to reappear, instead of thinking that you no longer exist.

☐ *Ticklishness* – from 6 months, babies start to become ticklish, although don't overdo the tickling games because your baby obviously can't say 'stop'.

WHEN TO WORRY

Check your baby's eyes and see your doctor if you notice any of the following – if vision problems are detected early, they are easier to treat:

- She doesn't fix on you or stare at your face
- She has a white or cloudy pupil, or the pupils don't look circular or equal in size, or don't get small in bright lights or bigger in dim lights
- Your baby's eyes don't follow you across the room
- Your baby's focus isn't straight most of the time – if her eyes point in different directions, this can indicate a squint. Remember, though, at this age the broad bridge across your baby's nose can make her look squinty, giving her a 'false squint', which she'll grow out of as her face gets bigger. Get her checked out all the same.

It's also worth seeing your doctor if your baby involuntarily drops objects after only a few moments, or if she can't grasp objects that fit easily into her fists. She may have a problem with motor development.

SAFETY TIP OF THE MONTH

Stay with your baby when she eats

Don't be tempted to pop out of the room when your baby is eating. Severe choking is silent, so watch your baby as she eats, don't rely on listening out for coughing. And for the same reason, don't leave her alone with a bottle of milk, even if she is now able to hold it by herself.

Also, don't 'help' your baby by putting a piece of food in her mouth. If she is unable to pick up and grasp the food by herself, it is thought that she won't be able to chew and swallow it. A baby's development keeps pace with her ability to manage food.

WHEN TO SEE THE DOCTOR

Choking

This is an inevitable part of weaning and something that parents dread. But nearly all babies will have a choking episode at some stage during weaning and there's little you can do to avoid it. It's possible to choke on anything – puree, milk, or even saliva.

What you can do is react competently when your child chokes. The other thing you can do is avoid foods which can get firmly lodged in the airway and cause severe choking, such as whole grapes or whole cherry tomatoes (these should always be cut in half). Another choking hazard is nuts, which shouldn't be given to children under 5 years old.

Also watch out for choking on long pieces of spaghetti or long strands of spinach or pak choi – pull these out of your child's mouth if they get stuck, or better still, cut them into small pieces beforehand.

ng

A baby's gag reflex is more easily triggered than an adult's, and can be triggered by a big bit of food – gagging is actually a protective mechanism to stop choking. Gagging is nothing to worry about – it looks a bit dramatic but your baby will quickly bring up the piece of food causing the problem.

Mild Choking

Your baby will be able to cry, breathe or cough during an episode of mild choking, and this will usually dislodge the food from her throat. All you can do is watch to make sure the choking doesn't get worse, and wait. Stay calm and your baby will be able to sort herself out. Afterwards your baby may seem a bit surprised, but probably won't be upset. You'll be in far more of a state, so try to calm your nerves and continue the meal.

Severe Choking

Sometimes your baby will be unable to dislodge a piece of food and so will be unable to cough or breathe. Silent choking is worrying; you need to lie her face down along your forearm with her head lower than her feet and bang her upper back five times. Check her mouth after each bang and see if you can see any obstruction – if you can, remove it.

If back blows don't work, try chest thrusts. Put your baby on her back then place two fingers in the middle of her chest and give five sharp thrusts, one every three seconds. The idea is to squeeze air up into her throat and dislodge the food.

Call an ambulance and continue to alternate banging her back with chest thrusts. If your baby loses consciousness, try banging her back again – it may work this time because the airways relax when you lose consciousness.

If it doesn't work, then you'll need to do resuscitation – book yourself on a first aid course if you haven't already done one; you'll feel more confident as a parent and may even save your child's life one day.

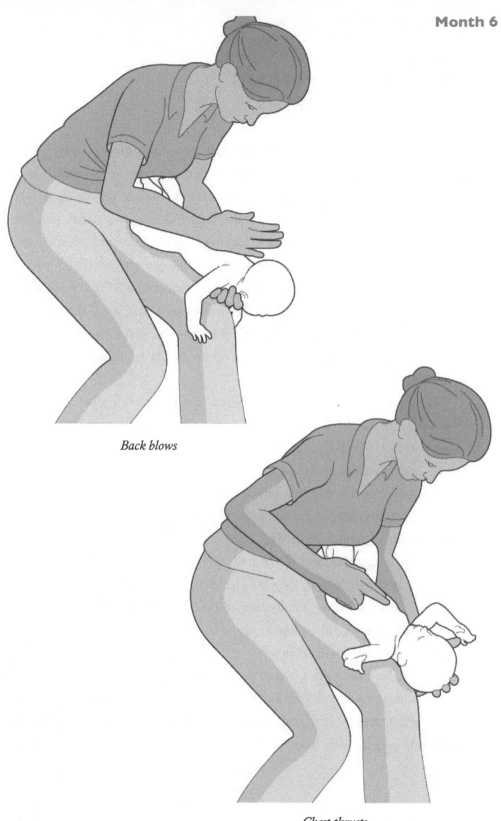

Back blows

Chest thrusts

WHAT'S HAPPENING TO MUM AND DAD

For many couples, this is the month when you move the cot out of your bedroom, because at 6 months the risk of cot death is vastly reduced. You'll feel a real sense of freedom as you switch on the main bedroom light, talk loudly, rustle newspapers and even watch telly. But most important, you can have sex without worrying about a sleeping baby in the corner of the room.

For many couples, having their bedroom back can give a rather dormant sex life a new lease of life. But you may find that you're STILL not having sex, and now you've no excuse. Well, don't panic just yet – if you went to a sex counsellor and said, 'We're not having much sex and we've got a 6-month-old baby,' he'd hardly throw up his hands in horror and suggest you're not right for each other!

It's incredibly common for post-baby sex to be rare or non-existent, and the reason is usually exhaustion. According to researchers at the Federal University of Sao Paulo, chronic sleep deprivation has an impact upon libido and could also be linked to erectile dysfunction.

Lack of sleep has also been linked with moodiness – so if you're snapping at each other and not getting on particularly well at the moment, then you're hardly going to want to have sex.

Plenty of couples have discovered, though, that if they have sex, even if they're not in the mood, they are pleasantly surprised by how much they enjoy it. So try booking a babysitter to take your baby to the park for an afternoon one weekend – three hours of sleep and sex will restore even the most exhausted bickering couples.

If you don't have the space to move your baby into her own room, you can console yourself with the fact that babies sleep more deeply as they get older, and it takes more to wake them. It's also another great reason to book an afternoon babysitter from time to time.

PLANNING AHEAD

Now that your baby is moving on to solids, it's time to go shopping. First, you'll need a highchair. Initially you can feed your baby by sitting her on your lap or putting her in her baby chair, but you'll need a highchair in a week or two when she starts getting more independent and messier.

A few things to think about when shopping for a highchair:

- How easy is it to clean?
- Does it fold up?
- Does the tray catch spills?
- Can you remove the tray and sit your baby at the family table?
- Can you strap your baby in securely (it won't be long before she is trying to stand up and escape)?

It's fine to buy a second-hand highchair, although you can get them new from around £25.

A recipe book is another good investment to give you lots of ideas for purees, finger foods and meals as your baby gets older.

If you are going down the puree route, you'll need to invest in a blender – you can buy a hand blender for less than £10 in supermarkets or Argos. To make larger quantities, you could invest in a food processor. To freeze the purees you'll need a flexible ice-cube tray, and freezer bags to put the frozen cubes into.

MONTH 7

INTRODUCTION

Sleep can be a big issue at around this time, because while some babies are now old enough to go through the night without waking up, plenty don't. So if you're still struggling on through broken nights and wondering if you'll ever get a solid eight hours' sleep again, you'll be pretty desperate for a solution.

Generally with babies there are no quick fixes, but there is an exception: controlled crying. This sleep technique nearly always gets fast results, and countless parents have rejoiced when after months of exhaustion they get their first unbroken night's sleep. This month is the ideal time to embark on this sleep-training method, and we'll talk you through how to do it and also offer gentler alternatives should you decide that controlled crying is not for you.

The other important issue this month is introducing your baby to finger food or lumpy food if you haven't done so already. If you delay this, you could have problems later on with a fussy baby who eats nothing but purees.

And if your baby wasn't quite ready for a highchair last month, she will almost certainly have the head control to sit in one this month, which gives you the green light for finger foods if you've not started them yet.

SLEEP

Aim: *uninterrupted night sleep 8–12 hours*
To bed early – about 7 or 8 p.m.
Two naps: *short (30- to 40-minute) morning nap, longer lunchtime nap (2–3 hours)*
A total of 14½ hours' sleep

In the early days when you were up most of the night, you probably assumed that by 6 months your baby would be sleeping easily through. And although it may seem as though everyone else's baby sleeps through, plenty of parents struggle for at least a year before their baby has an unbroken night's sleep.

If you're one of the struggling parents, there's plenty you can do to teach your baby to sleep better at night.

You will no doubt have learned lots of techniques to get your baby off to sleep by now – perhaps rocking, singing, sshhing or stroking her tummy. You may even be in the habit of driving your baby round the block to soothe her to sleep, or lying down with your baby to get her off.

Well, if you want your life back, you need to know that the less effort it takes to get your baby to sleep, the better. What you're aiming at is to teach your baby to fall asleep by herself if she is to get through the night – we all wake several times during the night, but most of us can get ourselves off to sleep again and don't even remember waking. Babies need to learn this, too.

There are two ways to teach this – either take a very gentle approach and slowly cut back on your soothing techniques until your baby eventually self-settles, or opt for the stricter 'controlled crying' approach, where you leave your baby to cry herself asleep and you don't give her any help at all.

Of course we would recommend starting with the more gentle approach. For many babies and parents this will work very well, although it may take at least a week to see an improvement and several months to get your baby sleeping through the night.

Plenty of parents choose controlled crying instead – often because their sanity, relationship, health and happiness have been pushed to the very edge by chronic sleep deprivation. If this sounds like you, then you may want to try controlled crying, which gets results within days.

The Gentle Approach

This looks very simple on the printed page, but in practice you will have to cut down on the help you give your baby, which means it will initially take her longer to go to sleep and so requires more time from you. If it used to take 10 minutes to rock your baby to sleep in your arms, it may now take 20 minutes of rubbing her tummy or stroking her hand while she lies in her cot. Or if you could sing your baby to sleep in 5 minutes, you may now have to spend 15 minutes sitting near the cot in silence while she falls asleep.

After a few weeks of this 'training', you can try walking around the bedroom but not paying attention to your baby, then you can progress to wandering in and out of the bedroom while she settles herself and knows you're near. Eventually you won't even have to be in the room. There will be crying during this process, but it's more likely to be short bouts of grizzling rather than full-blown howls.

The main message here is to tone down what you've been doing to get your baby to sleep until you're able to kiss her goodnight and then leave the room to let her fall asleep on her own without fuss.

Controlled Crying

This is a short, sharp sleep-training method, and your baby's total crying time will almost certainly be less than if you opt for the gentle approach involving small bouts of crying over several months.

This training is, however, quite harrowing for most parents as babies will often cry for at least an hour, though it only takes about three nights to complete. Some experts say that you can go in every 5 minutes because your baby will be comforted by seeing you, and plenty of parents have found this to be an effective but less harsh way of doing controlled crying. In our experience, however, if you've reached a point where you feel you need to do controlled crying, your baby will probably be very used to getting a lot of attention throughout the night. So we think you'll probably need a more drastic version of controlled crying to break the pattern. We've found that going in every 5 minutes can seem like teasing to some babies who will be frantic to be lifted out of the cot, and will then become more upset than ever when they realize this isn't going to happen as they watch you leave the room. So staying out of the room actually works better for some babies.

Interestingly, this method is often advised at sleep clinics, where they see the most desperate cases of baby-sleep problems.

We'd always suggest using controlled crying as a very last resort, but once you've decided to do it, then be committed. It's very tough and you'll feel guilty and upset listening to your baby cry herself to sleep. But don't be tempted to give in after half an hour, because if you do you'll be back to square one and the whole process will take even longer should you decide to start again.

Before you begin, ensure that your baby is well and doesn't have a fever (temperature over 38°C), that she isn't in pain or teething, and that she isn't hungry or thirsty. If your baby is suffering in any way there is no chance of getting her to sleep, and not feeding a hungry baby can lead to dehydration, which is why you shouldn't even think about controlled crying until your baby is at least 5 months old. Around 7 months is a particularly good age for trying this method, because you can be pretty sure that your baby isn't hungry but just wakes in the night for comfort feeds. Also, separation anxiety hasn't yet started – this begins in a couple of months and would, if you waited until then, make the training more stressful for your baby (and you!).

Ensure you have the support of your partner, because once you've kissed your baby goodnight, you'll need to leave her to cry herself to sleep and this is very tough on everyone. You'll probably find that your baby cries more on the second night, but you will see an improvement on night three. By night four, your baby will probably settle herself.

If your baby has been waking throughout the night to feed, you could try controlled crying for one feed at a time. Perhaps you could start with the midnight feed, then after a few nights move on to, say, the 4 a.m. feed. You'll find that your baby will learn more quickly with subsequent feeds, and may only take a night or two to learn to settle herself.

We suggest starting on a Friday night, then hopefully on night three, Sunday, your baby will sleep better before you and/or your partner has to return to work on Monday.

Troubleshooting

She doesn't want her daytime naps any more
Babies at this age are very sociable, and some will start to resent having to go for a quiet nap during the day because they think they are missing out. It's possible that your baby is becoming less tired now that she's a little older, in which case you could think about cutting or shortening her morning nap. But do persist with her lunchtime nap because most babies need this right up until the age of around 3. It may take longer than it used to to soothe your baby, but it's worth putting in a little effort to keep her napping habit. You may find she grizzles for 10 minutes before dropping off – your nerves will be on edge while you wait for your baby to sleep, but this phase will soon pass. As your baby gets older and more mobile, she'll be more willing to have her daytime nap.

She doesn't like early nights
It doesn't actually matter what time you put your baby to bed each night, but it should be at around the same time, give or take half an hour. This will help set your baby's body clock so she knows when it's time to sleep. And a

bedtime routine will help mentally prepare her for sleep (more on bedtime routines next month).

The advantage of an early night, around 7 p.m., is that you and your partner will have the evening to yourselves. But if you've gone back to work you may like to see your baby before she goes to bed, in which case you may want to set her bedtime slightly later.

It's easy enough to reset your baby's bedtime according to what works for your family – just think, the clocks change twice a year and it takes most young families just a day or two to adjust.

Once you've decided on a bedtime, you'll find that your baby soon needs to sleep at around this time each night. If she seems particularly alert it may well be because she has become overtired, which increases adrenaline levels, making her feel awake but also quite fretful. So don't put her to bed too long after her bedtime to avoid her becoming overtired.

FEEDING

Aim: by the end of the month your baby should be having two to three meals a day, including iron-rich foods. She will also be able to cope with lumpy and roughly mashed food, and not spit it out. And she will continue to experiment with and perhaps eat some finger foods. She could be on as few as three milk feeds a day – early morning, after lunch, and at bedtime. But don't worry too much if she still has more milk than this, as long as she's not having milk at night (see Month 6, 'Dropping the Night-feed').

You'll notice that your baby is becoming more dexterous and better able to pick up foods. By the end of the month she will probably be eating bigger quantities and so be able to cut down on her milk intake and drop some feeds until she is just having milk first thing in the morning, after lunch, and before bed. (If you're doing baby-led weaning your baby may not drop any milk feeds at all just yet if she's still mainly playing with her food.)

You may well leave purees behind this month as some babies start rejecting spoon-feeding from around now – others don't object until later (see Month 10), and some babies never seem to mind at all.

Why Lumpy Food Is Important

If your baby is happy to be spoon-fed, start to make her food lumpy because lots of babies get stuck on purees and refuse anything more challenging. This can be a difficult problem to resolve, but as long as you introduce lumps and finger food around now, it won't be an issue. The key is to do it gradually so that your baby hardly notices the change.

To make food lumpy you can add soft cooked peas, chopped cooked carrot or tiny pasta shapes (you can buy baby pasta from pharmacies, but it's cheaper to buy tiny pasta shells, called conchigliette, from supermarkets). Mashing food rather than pureeing it makes food lumpier, and not pureeing food too finely is a good idea, too.

Is It OK to Use Jars of Baby Food?

There's no doubt that jars of baby food are very convenient, especially when you're out and about. But we don't recommend using jars exclusively because the puree (in the jars formulated for 4-month-olds) is so smooth that some babies find it too much of a shock when lumps are introduced (in the 7-month jars), so they spit everything out and refuse to eat. Making your own purees allows you to make your baby's food thicker and lumpier very gradually.

The other downside with jars is that the food is heat-treated, which gives it a different taste that some babies get used to and then refuse to eat anything else, including family food. Also, relying on jars alone can be expensive.

We suggest using jars for the times when you haven't planned a meal and need to feed your baby quickly, or if you're going out and don't know if you'll be able to feed your baby easily.

There's no need to warm jars up – if you get your baby used to cold food from jars it will make them even more convenient. Also, if you haven't warmed the food you can put the unfinished jar in the fridge to be eaten later – but always within 24 hours.

Allergies

This is a fast developing area and, as a result, weaning methods have changed massively in the last few years. Until recently parents would often introduce foods to their babies in a particular order, starting with very bland vegetables or fruits, then gradually exposing them to things like meat, fish, dairy, eggs and wheat – all the time keeping an eye out for signs of allergy.

But you can forget this painstaking regime because current advice tells parents to introduce all foods to their babies when they start weaning at 6 months (just avoiding things like whole nuts, which are a choking hazard). The European Food Safety Authority states that there is no convincing evidence that avoiding or delaying the introduction of potentially allergenic foods has any effect in reducing the risk of developing allergies. And ongoing research shows that excluding foods may actually *increase* the likelihood of allergies.

It's a similar story with peanuts – you may have heard that you should avoid giving children under 3 years old foods containing peanuts if there is a family history of allergy. Now the latest research tells us that there's no clear evidence this will reduce the risk of your child developing a peanut allergy. The number of UK schoolchildren with nut allergies has doubled in the last decade despite previous guidelines, and nut allergies are extremely low in countries where peanuts form part of a weaned baby's diet. So you can relax about giving your baby peanut butter unless you have a specific concern, in which case speak to your GP.

Parents who decide to wean early shouldn't introduce wheat until 6 months because of the risk of your baby developing coeliac disease. (See Month 9, When to See the Doctor, for more on coeliac disease.)

DEVELOPMENT AND PLAY

Talking

Lots of babies really find their voice this month, and will not only love babbling away to themselves, but will also learn to shout for attention. So instead of crying when she wants or doesn't want something, your baby may shout instead – for example if she wants something you're eating.

Your baby is still too young to wave hello, but if she sees someone she recognizes and likes she may wave with both hands and her legs too, and she'll smile with sheer delight.

If you're not in the habit of calling your baby by her name, then start now because she's old enough to recognize it – she'll soon start to respond when she hears her name.

MILESTONES

(All babies are different – you probably won't be able to tick everything on this list.)

☐ *Head lift* – when your baby is lying on her back, she will start to lift her head and shoulders to look around.

☐ *Raking objects towards her* – when your baby is on her tummy she will try not only to reach for a toy, but will try to rake it towards herself.

☐ *Two-handed grasp* – your baby will start to grasp toys and food and pass them from hand to hand this month, but will still be clumsy and drop things. So give her soft toys to play with such as fabric bricks and dolls rather than the plastic versions – this means that if she's on her back and drops a toy onto her head, or she's on her tummy and swipes her face with a toy, she won't hurt herself.

☐ *One toy at a time* – if your baby is holding, say, a red brick and you pass her a blue one, she'll drop the red one before being able to take the blue one.

☐ *Wanting to 'get down'* – you may find that your baby wants to get down from your arms or lap if you are holding her – she'll let you know by arching her back. Also, she may not like sitting in her baby chair any more – it will suddenly seem restrictive to her now that she's learning to move. This can be quite inconvenient, because it's useful to have your baby safely and happily bouncing in her chair, but it's important that you give her lots of 'tummy time' to build her muscles.

☐ *Crawling* – most babies start crawling at between 7 and 10 months old, so some babies will start around now. She will need good head control as well as strong arms and legs. And lots of babies crawl backwards before they can crawl forwards. This is because they learn to coordinate their arms *before* their legs. Some babies never crawl at all but will bottom-shuffle and go straight from sitting to walking.

☐ *Bouncing* – if you stand your baby on your knee she will now take her weight in her legs and 'bounce' as she flexes and extends her knees.

☐ *Searching* – now that your baby has developed object permanence, she is able to start searching for objects that she can't actually see (instead of assuming that they don't exist). So try putting a toy, partly hidden under a cloth, in front of her and ask your baby, 'Where's it gone?' She'll feel proud and excited that she knows. Then after a few weeks you can progress to hiding a toy under a cup so that it's not visible at all.

WHEN TO WORRY

If your baby isn't able to pass an object from hand to hand by the end of this month, it may mean that her fine motor skills are slow to develop, so it's worth seeing your doctor about this.

SAFETY TIP OF THE MONTH

Watch out for your baby falling down the stairs

By now most babies are able to roll, some will be creeping, a few will be starting to crawl, and some will be shuffling along on their bottoms. It's very common for babies to fall down the stairs, and while most will be lucky enough to avoid broken bones or head injuries, it's essential to be vigilant because stairs pose a very real risk to babies and young children.

In Month 10 we talk about how to teach your baby to crawl down the stairs, but in the meantime, take extra care. If you're planning to get a stair gate then now's the time to do so, although do ensure that it's securely in place, and don't forget to keep it closed.

WHEN TO SEE THE DOCTOR ✚

Glue Ear

We covered this in our first book, *Your Baby Week by Week*, but we feel it is worth another mention because one in five children will suffer from glue ear at some stage. It's important that this condition is picked up, because it causes hearing loss which affects language development.

Glue ear is mainly found in toddlers but affects some babies, too, peaking in the under-2s between the ages of 6 and 10 months. It occurs when the Eustachian tube, which connects the middle ear to the back of the throat, becomes blocked. As a result, sticky fluid blocks the middle ear, making hearing difficult (like listening underwater) and it can also cause pain.

Babies are more prone to glue ear if you or your partner smoke – but any baby can be affected, so do be aware of the signs.

The main symptom is hearing loss, so look for signs like your baby not noticing you coming into the room, or not turning when you speak. Perhaps she doesn't seem to enjoy you making funny noises and 'talking' with her as much as she used to.

Because glue ear can sometimes cause pain, do look out for your baby tugging at her ears or rubbing them. It's worth noting that glue ear has nothing to do with ear wax – if your baby has lots of wax, this is *not* an indication of glue ear.

Your doctor will examine your baby's ears and arrange a hearing test. Most specialists will suggest waiting 3 months to see if your baby's glue ear clears up by itself. If your baby isn't in pain and glue ear is affecting hearing only in one ear, then your doctor will continue to monitor her. But if her hearing is affected significantly or she's in pain, your baby will probably be referred to an ear, nose and throat specialist who may put her on a course of steroid nasal drops.

After the age of 1, your baby may be given grommets – minor surgery to insert tiny tubes that pierce the ear drum to release pressure. The operation is done under general anaesthetic as a day case and instantly improves hearing. The grommets usually drop out by themselves within 6 to 18 months, by which time your baby will hopefully have grown out of glue ear.

WHAT'S HAPPENING TO MUM AND DAD

You may have managed to get out with your partner for special occasions such as birthdays and perhaps even a wedding or party on your own. Grandparents have probably been very willing to step in and help. But low-key dates such as going to the pub or cinema tend to vanish once you have children. Find a babysitter you can trust, if you haven't done so already.

The beauty of local dates is that they are just that – local. So you can be on your mobile and home within 15 minutes if necessary. The other advantage is that you'll only be out a couple of hours, which keeps babysitting costs to a minimum, and getting back early means you won't be shattered the next day.

Now is a very good time to get your baby used to new babysitters before separation anxiety begins – when babies become clingy and want to be with Mum rather than people they don't know. This can start as early as 9 months, so it's well worth introducing a new babysitter sooner rather than later.

For the same reason, if you're planning to go back to work around now, or have already gone back, you'll find it easier than in a few months' time because your baby will happily go to a kindly stranger and won't appear to miss you in the slightest.

If you don't have to go back to work just yet, you will need to take separation anxiety into account when you organize your childcare – we shall cover this in Month 11, just before separation anxiety peaks.

PLANNING AHEAD

Child Backpack

If you and your partner love the outdoors, you could think about buying a baby backpack to carry your child around in on walks. These are good for trekking where it's difficult to take the buggy – for instance off the beaten track and on sandy or pebbly beaches – and your baby is now old enough to be able to sit up in one without her head wobbling around too much.

Look for something with a rain cover, and ideally both front and rear headrests to allow your baby to sleep if she wants to. The front headrest – a small padded flap in front of the baby – will allow her to safely slump forward when sleeping instead of continually bumping into your head. We've found this is often the position babies in backpacks adopt when dozing.

Obviously try on the backpack before buying to make sure it's comfortable – your baby will seem very heavy after an hour or so of plodding along a rocky beach or up a mountain trail. Well-padded straps are a must, and good backpacks have padded hip supports and a waist belt to spread the load – much like a proper hiking rucksack.

Find one that has openable legs so that it'll stand securely on the ground by itself without risk of toppling over, and some built-in storage space for food and drink is also handy. While costs can vary enormously, for occasional use a moderately priced backpack is fine, or look for a good second-hand one (but check there's no undue wear on the straps and buckles). Dedicated hikers may want to splash out on a more rugged and weatherproof model.

Playpen

If you've got the space, playpens are useful for popping your baby into if you need to answer the door, go to the toilet or carry a hot dish of food out of the oven. They also work well with subsequent children – you can put a newborn in a playpen knowing he is safe from older siblings.

It's a good idea to get your baby used to a playpen before she becomes mobile – then she won't object too much later on. So long as there are some favourite toys in the playpen, your baby will be happy playing in it for a while.

It can be tempting to dump your baby in the playpen knowing she's safe while you have a bit of a break, especially when she becomes more mobile, but it's important to let her out when she wants or the pen will seem more like a prison to her.

MONTH 8

INTRODUCTION

Your baby will be offered her 8-month health review around now – this can be done any time between 6 months and a year. Either your GP or a health visitor or nurse will carry out a routine check to ensure that your baby is developing within the normal range. Don't forget your baby's red book, because she will be weighed and her length will be measured. The health professional will also check her sight, movement and whether she can babble, and ask about your baby's feeding and sleeping habits. Finally, you will be asked about your own emotional and physical wellbeing – plenty of parents find themselves struggling for one reason or another, so this is a good opportunity to get some support.

The most common things to be picked up during this check include hearing and sight problems as well as any general development delays.

If you haven't been offered a routine check yet, contact your GP or see a health visitor at your local baby clinic. The UK Government has published guidelines stating that all babies should receive a second general health review (the first one is at 6 weeks) before their first birthday, so you are well within your rights to ask for this check.

SLEEP

Aim: uninterrupted night sleep 8–12 hours
To bed early – about 7 or 8 p.m.
Two naps: short (30- to 40-minute) morning nap, longer lunchtime nap (2–3 hours)
A total of 14½ hours' sleep

We've mentioned a bedtime routine in previous chapters, and you no doubt have some sort of routine in place. Every family has their own rituals at bedtime; the general idea is to spend about an hour after dinner calming your baby before sleep.

The key is to keep it soothing, and one of the ways you can do this is to keep bedtime the same every night – babies and young children are comforted by the predictability of a routine. As well as a bath, milk and perhaps a massage, your routine can now include a story, because your baby is old enough to enjoy looking at the pictures with you.

Try to avoid television in the last couple of hours before sleep, as this can have a stimulating effect on the brain and prevent sleepiness. Ideally babies shouldn't watch any television at all before the age of 2 – more on this in Month 20.

When it comes to finally saying goodnight, we suggest that you pop your baby in her cot, give her a quick kiss, say goodnight and leave her room. Your aim should be to make your departure short, sharp and identical each night so that your baby knows exactly what to expect. Then when separation anxiety begins, probably in a few months' time, your baby will be less likely to start getting anxious when you leave the room. We talk more about separation anxiety in Months 10 and 16.

Troubleshooting

Baby wriggling out of covers

My baby wriggles out of her covers to the top of her cot, then wakes up cold

New babies need to be put to sleep in the foot-to-foot position, which means that their feet are down by the foot of the cot. The idea is that if they wriggle they will move to the top end of the cot and won't get trapped under the blankets. Yes, they may get cold, but this obviously isn't so serious. Once your baby is mobile, you can put her to bed with her head at the top end of the cot because she is strong enough not to get stuck under the covers. The advantage is that she is less likely to wake up cold. The other way around this problem is to use a baby sleeping bag.

My baby wakes at 6 every morning

Some babies are naturally early risers, and plenty of parents simply accept that their baby's day starts at around 6 a.m. This can go on well into toddler and pre-school years, and the trick is to teach your baby to play happily in her cot while the rest of the household has a bit more sleep.

Leave a few toys and books at the end of your baby's cot for her to 'discover' in the morning (avoid anything she can hurt herself on such as pull-along-toys with strings that she could wrap around her neck). This will probably keep her happy for a good 20 minutes, and you'll find that you may be able to stretch this to 40 minutes before she becomes either bored or hungry.

Go to your baby once she starts crying for attention, but try to avoid feeding her earlier than her usual breakfast time or you will reset her hunger clock to start earlier.

My baby used to sleep well but has started waking at 5 a.m.

If your baby is waking earlier than 6 a.m., which is quite common at this age, then we suggest you try to resolve this rather than feeling obliged to start your day while it's still dark.

Babies tend to sleep lightly in the early morning and can be woken by hunger or pain. So work out if your baby is hungry – perhaps she drank less milk or ate less than usual the previous day. Also ask yourself if she could be teething, or perhaps she's getting a cold.

If this is the case, then the early morning waking will soon pass because your baby will naturally eat more in a day or so, and teething and colds get better.

Sometimes babies get into the habit of dawn awakenings even once the teething or cold has passed. To break this habit you can soothe your baby back to sleep in order to reset her body clock not to wake at dawn. It will seem challenging as you sing or rock her, all the while wondering if you will get back to bed again or if your day has already begun. But if you can get your baby back to sleep, even for half an hour, it will make a difference to resetting her body clock.

You won't get her back to sleep every morning, but persevere, because after about a week your baby won't be waking up quite so early.

Controlled crying won't work after about 5 a.m. because your baby will have had plenty of sleep so will have masses of energy to cry for a good hour or two, and by about 7 a.m. it will be time for her breakfast. This will give a very confusing message: 'Cry for two hours and you get breakfast.'

She rolls onto her front when she sleeps – what about cot death?
Some babies roll over and sleep on their fronts around now. You don't need to roll your baby onto her back again – the risk of cot death is greatly reduced by this age. You'll actually find that your baby sleeps much better on her front, especially if she tucks her knees up under herself – this seems to ease indigestion. Also she won't wake herself with the morrow reflex – this is a normal baby reflex which makes babies fling their arms and legs out, and can wake them up. They grow out of this by the age of 1. But do continue to put your baby to sleep on her back – it's up to her if she rolls over or not.

FEEDING

Aim: by the end of the month your baby should be having three meals a day, including two iron-rich foods a day. She will probably be coping well with lumps, getting better at eating finger foods, and hopefully having just three to four milk feeds a day.

This month, continue to encourage your baby to drop milk feeds to just three a day – first thing in the morning, after lunch, and at bedtime. It's quicker and easier for babies to get calories from milk than from solids, and sometimes older babies choose to fill up on milk, which can be problematic as they then don't have an appetite for their meals.

For breastfeeding mums, this is a very natural way to slowly cut down. Your breasts may feel a little 'full' for a day or so as you skip a particular feed, and you may have extra milk at the next feed for a few days, resulting in your baby wanting fewer solids. But this will soon settle.

You can continue to breastfeed for as long as you and your baby are happy. Lots of women will have stopped by now, and some will stop at a year – perhaps because they want to be able to go out for an entire evening and leave someone else to do the bedtime feed.

Others continue to breastfeed well into their baby's second year – the early morning feed is an easy one to keep going because, unless you are away for the night, you'll be able to feed your baby. Lots of mums love snuggling up with their babies in the early hours, especially if they have gone back to work.

The More Mess, the Better

Around now you may notice that your baby seems to be making more mess than ever at mealtimes, squeezing her spaghetti and smearing scrambled egg over her face and hair. This is a good sign, indicating that she is enjoying her food, but more importantly that you are allowing her to play with her food and aren't desperately trying to keep things clean. The messier the better as far as your baby is concerned – she doesn't know it's a pain to clean up after her, she's just having a wonderful time learning new eating skills.

If the mess is really getting to you, we suggest setting aside one meal a day where you give her difficult-to-clear-up foods and don't try to wipe up until she's finished. For her other two meals you could give her 'cleaner' foods such as sandwiches. But again, try to resist cleaning up before she's finished, especially wiping her hands and face throughout her meal.

Beware of the Bottle

Your baby will be able to hold her own bottle from around now. But resist the temptation to leave her in her cot with a bottle of formula while she settles herself to sleep. While this is an easy shortcut, it's bad for her teeth because she'll fall asleep with her teeth in a pool of sweet liquid (milk contains lactose, a sugar). This will be a tough habit to break later on.

Vitamin Drops

If you are breastfeeding or your baby is drinking fewer than 500ml of formula a day, the UK Department of Health recommends you give your baby vitamins A, C and D. You can buy NHS Healthy Start children's vitamin drops from chemists (£1.77), or you can get them free if you are on Income Support. Speak to your health visitor or visit www.healthystart.nhs.uk.

The Department of Health also recommends that breastfeeding women take a vitamin D supplement – again, you can buy NHS Healthy Start vitamins for women (77p) – these are free if you are on Income Support and breastfeeding a baby under 1 year.

(These vitamins are more expensive in Scotland – £2.27 and £1.77 respectively.)

DEVELOPMENT AND PLAY

Talking

This month your baby may start to watch your lips and mouth closely when you talk, and will be fascinated by the movement and maybe even copy you.

She will also start to experiment with sounds, making high- and low-pitched noises. She will produce short syllables such as 'da' and 'ba' or 'baba', and may start to combine different consonants when babbling, such as 'maba'.

The most common babbling sounds include: 'b', 'p', 'm', 't', 'd', 'k' and 'g'. Most of the time babies of this age don't have meaning attached to the sounds they make; it's more about experimenting with their mouth and voice. But your baby will still use these sounds to try and 'talk' to you, and it's important that you respond to her attempts to communicate – so have fun making conversation together. (More on responding to your baby in Month 9.)

Your baby will recognize and respond to her name around now, and if you ask, 'Where's Daddy?' she may turn her head towards him – she'll do the same for other familiar people, pets, or objects.

You can start 'reading' together now, if you haven't already done so. Your baby will be given a Bookstart pack during her developmental check (see Planning Ahead, page 52, for details). You can also buy a selection of baby books or borrow them from the library – you won't be charged if you bring books back late or if your baby damages them. Pictures of animals, babies and familiar objects are usually popular at this age, as are 'touch books' with different textures or holes for your baby to explore with her hands. Reading together will develop your baby's memory, imagination, language and concentration.

As well as reading as part of the bedtime routine, you can also read to your baby during the day to calm her down if ever she's a bit fretful. A reading break and a cuddle will refresh her and hopefully put her in a better mood.

MILESTONES

(All babies are different – you probably won't be able to tick everything on this list.)

☐ *Better concentration* – you may notice that your baby is able to concentrate on toys and other objects this month, and will be happy to spend time examining things closely.

☐ *Holding a cup* – as her coordination continues to improve, your baby will be able to hold her own cup or bottle (if she's bottle-fed). She'll also be able to bang her hands, perhaps on her highchair tray, or on a table.

☐ *Stomping on your knee* – instead of bouncing by bending her knees, your baby will start to stomp each foot as she prepares for walking.

☐ *Standing* – when you stand your baby on your knee or the floor, she'll be less wobbly this month and may keep her legs straight as you hold her weight.

☐ *Swinging at the park* – you could try putting your baby on a baby-swing at the park this month and pushing her very gently. After a few times she'll probably squeal with delight and kick her legs in excitement. If she still seems a bit wobbly, leave it a few weeks – after all, there's no rush.

☐ *Letting go* – if you ask your baby for a toy she may be able to cooperate and let go of it – before she will have found it difficult to deliberately let go of an object.

WHEN TO WORRY

As your baby becomes mobile you may notice that she seems to use her right or left side preferentially. This could be due to cerebral palsy, which makes a baby stiff or floppy on one side so she will have difficulty using this side. It can also be a sign of problems with peripheral vision if she reaches out only to one side.

SAFETY TIP OF THE MONTH

Set the hot water thermostat low enough so that your baby can't scald herself in the bath if she plays with the taps. Depending on what sort of central heating system you've got and how it's set up, the hot water temperature control may be on the boiler itself or could be a separate thermostat control, usually on the hot water cylinder if you've got one.

It's also good practice always to run the cold water into the bath first, before the hot, so that the bath water is never scalding or uncomfortably hot. You can also buy a non-slip bath mat if your child is able to sit up in the bath and no longer needs a bath chair.

WHEN TO SEE THE DOCTOR ✚

Intussusception

This is when the bowel folds inside itself, causing an obstruction. Signs include bloody diarrhoea, or stools that resemble redcurrant jelly. Your baby will have intense spasms of pain, perhaps drawing her knees up to her chest. She may also have a swollen tummy and vomiting. Intussusception is most common about two months after a baby goes on to solids, at about 8 months. It happens when food causes swelling in the *Peyer's patches*, a type of lymph node in the bowel. This makes the bowel fold in on itself like a collapsed telescope.

The condition is rare, however, affecting between one and four in 1,000 babies, and is three times more common in boys than girls.

Urgent treatment is essential, so take your baby to your hospital's emergency department if you're concerned. A doctor will feel your baby's tummy for a 'sausage-shaped mass' and probably order an X-ray or ultrasound. If your baby is very ill and the doctors suspect damage to the intestine, they will operate immediately. Otherwise they will do a barium enema using a catheter in the rectum to confirm the diagnosis and also to try and cure the problem – the pressure from the enema often unfolds the bowel. If this procedure isn't successful, your child will be offered surgery.

WHAT'S HAPPENING TO MUM AND DAD

If you've been a mum on maternity leave, you may well have been the one getting up in the night for baby feeds, especially if you were breastfeeding. But if you go back to work you'll no doubt want to renegotiate – also, your baby has probably more or less stopped night-feeds by now.

The textbook solution is to sit down together and have a reasonable discussion about who should do what. But the reality is often that your baby wakes in the middle of the night and you both play 'deaf', pretending to be asleep and hoping that the other one will get up.

In an ideal world you'd be sensitive to each other's needs and would kindly volunteer to get up if you knew your partner was particularly tired for one reason or another, but exhaustion can make the sweetest-natured parents ruthlessly selfish when it comes to sleep. A realistic solution is to either take turns whenever your baby wakes up ('I got up last time so you get up this time'), or take turns being 'on duty' each night – if your baby sleeps through on your night you'll feel lucky, but if she wakes continually with, say, teething pain, you'll be shattered – but at least you'll get a good night's sleep the following night. The key is to share responsibilities so you both get some regular rest.

PLANNING AHEAD

You may need to think about replacing your baby's car seat, because lots of seats for newborns are only suitable from birth to about 9 months or 10kg in weight. You don't have to wait until your baby weighs 10kg, though, because the next-stage car seat is actually suitable from 9 to 18kg, about 9 months to 4 years.

Some babies become quite fractious during car journeys at about this age and it can often be because they are starting to get too big for their seat and feel uncomfortable. With any luck your baby will soon settle down again when she gets her new, more comfortable seat.

Having said that, babies should remain in rear-facing car seats for as long as possible, because this is a safer way to travel. Some seats are suitable up to 13kg – check the label on yours, and also make sure that your baby's head doesn't stick over the top of her seat.

You could think about buying another rear-facing car seat. These are still quite unusual in the UK, but evidence from Sweden shows they give children more protection.

Which? magazine (www.which.co.uk) regularly tests baby and child seats, checking for the best performance in simulated crashes, and also looking at ease of installation. The website is subscription only, but you can get a month's trial subscription for just £1.

This month you can also look out for your Bookstart pack, which is usually given out to 7- to 9-month-old babies by health visitors. Or you can collect a pack from your local library. This nationwide scheme provides free books to all babies; the pack contains a canvas bag, two board books, a laminated rhyme sheet and a leaflet on sharing books with your baby. See www.bookstart.org.uk for more details.

MONTH 9

INTRODUCTION

Between the ages of 9 and 12 months your baby will go through incredible changes, and may well start either walking or talking. Initially she will put more effort into one or the other of these skills, and this month you will probably see if she is going to be an early walker or an early talker. There's a loose pattern for girls to be earlier talkers, and for boys to be better at crawling and walking – but of course this isn't always the case.

Babies who are destined to be early walkers will be crawling this month – some will pull themselves up to standing, and a few will take their first steps. Early walkers are often brave beyond their capabilities and fall over a lot, which means you have to watch them more closely than ever. But the upside is that, in the initial stages, their new skills are more obvious and impressive than those of early talkers, who may utter the beginnings of a word, but rarely do so on command. The exceptionally early talkers may say the beginning of a word, for example 'ca' for 'cat', and this will be followed in the next few weeks by their first word.

Of course most babies won't be 'exceptionally' early walkers or talkers, and you'll probably have to wait another month or two for anything much to happen in these developmental stages. Do bear in mind, too, that it's developmentally normal not to talk until well over a year, or walk until 18 months – so you may be in for a long wait!

The average age for walking is actually later than it used to be, since the 'back to sleep' campaign of putting babies to sleep on their backs to reduce the risk of cot death. Babies don't build up muscles as quickly on their backs as when they are on their fronts, and whereas babies used to walk at about 11 or 12 months on average, these days it tends to be between 12 and 15 months.

Don't worry if your baby doesn't seem to be 'keeping up'. We have included signs to watch out for that can indicate developmental problems in our 'when to worry' boxes, so hopefully you can make a few quick checks then get on and enjoy your baby without obsessing over her development.

Do note that there will be quite a lot of friendly pressure from well-meaning friends and relatives asking if your baby is saying anything yet or if she's walking. Don't get sucked in to the crazy baby race. The more you learn to quell your competitive streak, the more you'll be able to relax with your child and have fun together. Babies aren't competitive and your little one won't mind in the slightest if she's the last of her peers to walk or talk – but she *will* notice if you're more uptight than usual.

SLEEP

Aim: uninterrupted night sleep 9–12 hours
To bed early – about 7 or 8 p.m.
One or two naps: *sometimes a short (20- to 30-minute) morning nap, plus a longer lunchtime nap (2–3 hours)*
A total of 14½ hours' sleep

As we all know, the biggest sleep issue for parents is whether or not your baby is sleeping through the night and, as previously mentioned, around 70 per cent of babies will be sleeping through by 9 months, according to the National Sleep Foundation. If this includes your baby, congratulations and welcome back to the world.

If you're still living in the land of foggy-headed days and broken nights, though, hang on in there. Your baby is still very young and trainable, so do refer back to our suggestions in Month 7.

It really is worth putting some effort into sleep-training at this stage, because research has found that encouraging babies to get to sleep on their own without your help reduces sleep problems when they are older. One particular study, published in the US journal *Pediatrics* in 2007, looked at nearly 2,000 children from when they were 5 months to 3½ years old. It found that if the mother stayed with her very young child at bedtime until he fell asleep, the child was more likely to refuse to go to bed at bedtime when he was older. The study also revealed that if a mother took her young child into her own bed, the child was more likely to continually wake during the night when he was older.

Troubleshooting

I'm finding it impossible to get my baby down for her morning nap
Some babies will start to drop their morning nap around now – this generally happens from 9 months to a year old, by which time most babies have one nap a day. Some babies don't drop this morning nap until about 18 months. If your baby doesn't want to have her morning sleep, let her skip this nap and perhaps put her down a little earlier at lunchtime if she seems tired.

It takes most babies a few weeks to drop a nap – they'll go for a couple of days without it, then suddenly need that sleep again to catch up. Just follow your baby's natural pattern and let her drop her nap in her own time.

The only time you might like to step in, however, is if your baby continues with her morning nap but stops sleeping for so long at lunchtime. Getting your baby into the habit of a long after-lunch snooze is important because she will continue to have this nap up until she is about 3. So we'd suggest waking her up a littler earlier from her morning nap to ensure that she is tired by lunchtime.

The other benefit of dropping a nap is that babies sometimes start to sleep for a bit longer at night.

My baby used to sleep through the night, but now wakes up
It's common for a baby's sleep pattern to regress at about this age, but if you've got her sleeping through before, it will be much easier to do so again.

The most likely reason at this age is teething or indigestion (your baby is still getting used to new foods). See 'When to See the Doctor' in Month 11 for more information on teething. If you think your baby gets indigestion – perhaps she wakes up with tummy pain which is relieved by passing wind – you could try to minimize the quantities of challenging foods such as pulses, onions and dried fruit, and also time them for earlier in the day. Give her more gentle foods at night. Some parents even switch breakfast and dinner for a few weeks – your baby won't know she's 'supposed to' eat porridge in the morning, and will happily have her 'dinner' first thing.

FEEDING

Aim: *from 9 months your baby should be eating three or four servings of carbohydrates a day such as rice, bread and potatoes, three to four servings of fruit and vegetables, and two servings of protein such as meat, fish, eggs, cheese or yoghurt. She should be having three meals a day, and she may be eating a couple of in-between snacks such as fruit or toast. Your baby should be drinking about a pint of formula or breastmilk (about 550ml) – two large feeds or three smaller feeds a day.*

You can use these guidelines until your baby is about 2 years old, when we recommend giving her more fruit and vegetables – see Month 23.

Your baby may really click with finger food this month as she will be more dexterous. She will develop her mature pincer movement around now, which allows her to pick up tiny bits of food such as blueberries (you can cut them in half), peas, beans, and even grains of rice.

Some babies will also be capable of 'dips' this month – dipping carrot batons, for example, into a puree of pork, orange juice and sweet potato. This is particularly useful if you are doing baby-led weaning, because dips, like purees, can pack in more calories and nutrients than finger foods.

Her Own Spoon

You can give your baby her own spoon this month. She'll make a mess and be very slow, but you can help her by loading the spoon then letting her hold it, perhaps with a bit of support. Let your baby try to guide it into her mouth so that she feels in charge of her eating.

If you let her practise with a spoon at least once a day, she'll get the hang of it in the next couple of months or so.

If your baby is eating well, then get her to try lots of different foods, particularly things like vegetables, liver, mackerel and anything that is healthy but that older kids may describe as 'yuk'. Most babies are adventurous with their food until they reach the age of 1, so make the most of the next few months.

Good Little Eater

Grandparents may well describe your baby as a 'good little eater' around now, as lots of babies at this age enjoy their food and are happy to try different things. Be prepared for all this to change, though, because in a few months most babies will start to become more selective, which will make feeding more challenging. This can be made worse by outside pressure from family and friends observing that your baby is no longer a 'good little eater'. Do try to ignore them, because when it comes to feeding babies and toddlers, the more relaxed you stay, the better. Remember, it's not a competition.

DEVELOPMENT AND PLAY

Talking

Your baby's understanding will increase this month, and she'll recognize a lot of what you say if it concerns her. For example, you could be discussing her rice cakes with someone else and your baby may suddenly sit forward and squeal because she wants one.

Your baby's ability to understand is actually far more important than her ability to talk, as far as assessing her development is concerned. So do keep chatting to your baby, even if she doesn't utter a single word until well into her second year.

Around now your baby will probably start to use gestures, and may start to point and grunt to indicate what she wants. This is your cue to respond. So if, say, she grunts and looks and points towards a banana, you can give it to her and say, 'Banana, here you are, is this what you want?' Because she has initiated the communication she is likely to memorize the word 'banana', and may recognize it when she hears it again, even though she won't say the word banana herself for a while yet.

Your baby may try to imitate sounds you make, such as sneezing, coughing or animal noises, for example 'moo' or 'quack'. You can repeat these sounds back to her and wait to see if she responds by laughing or vocalizing again.

If she's going to be an early talker, she might say the beginning of a word, perhaps 'mama' and 'dada'. It's worth knowing that it's easier to say the sound 'da' than 'ma', which is why lots of babies end up saying 'dada' before 'mama' – it's not favouritism. Interestingly, babies tend to make a pitiful 'maaaa' sound when they are crying, but a cheerful 'da, da' sound when happy.

But do note that 'ma' and 'da' are both quite easy consonants for babies to vocalize, and if she happens to say 'ma' and gets a big reaction from you, she's bound to say it again.

In fact, your response to your baby's gestures, babble and 'talking' is fundamental to her learning to speak. If you smile and talk back when your baby 'says' something, she will be more likely to 'say' it again.

Reading together is a good opportunity to respond to your baby. Mostly, she will be happy to sit in silence and listen, but when she does want to point at something or perhaps 'babble' about the pictures, do make a point of listening and responding to her contribution.

MILESTONES

(All babies are different – you probably won't be able to tick everything on this list.)

☐ *Pointing* – once she can use her index finger with precision, she'll be able to point. Babies start pointing with their arm, then manage to do so with their index finger.

☐ *Cooperation* – some babies will understand what you want them to do this month, and start to cooperate. For example, if you're dressing your baby she may help to put her arms through the arm holes. Or she may hold out her hands to be dried.

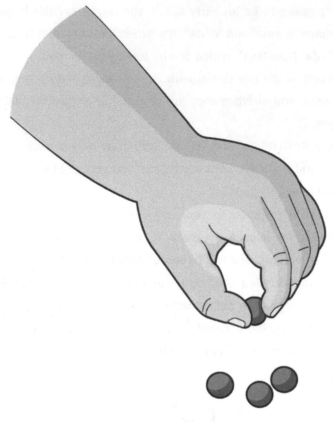

Pincer grip

☐ *Mature pincer grip* – this month your baby may start to use her thumb and forefinger to pick up objects (instead of using all her fingers in a claw-like way). This will enable her to pick up tiny objects such as peas. Also she'll be able to play with more intricate toys and have great fun tearing up newspapers.

☐ *Standing up* – your baby may pull herself to stand up for a few wobbly seconds this month, although most babies don't do this until 11 months.

Babies who stand early may demand help to sit down again, which can take its toll on your nerves. Late standers are usually better able to lower themselves gently back onto their bottoms. Don't keep making her stand if she's not ready to do it on her own yet, as she'll get tired. You can't speed up how quickly she learns to stand and walk, and some babies won't stand up until well after their first birthday. But a sign that she isn't far off is that her feet are flat on the floor – rather than curling – when you hold her in the standing position.

☐ *Following your gaze* – this month your baby will be able to follow your gaze if you look at something and point. So you can start to point out cats, dogs, fire engines, diggers – anything fun or unusual.

☐ *Looking across the room* – your baby's vision will be better than ever now, and she'll be able see up to 4 metres away. This means that she can recognize you across the room, and she'll be very interested in looking out of the car window and her buggy. She'll probably want to sit upright in her buggy, and may want to lean forward to get a good view of the world.

☐ *Interested in cause-and-effect toys* – your baby will start to appreciate toys such as a jack-in-the-box – wind the handle and something happens. You may need to help her with such toys and she'll want you to repeat the action many times, but she'll love the anticipation.

☐ *Anticipating* – towards the end of this month your baby may be able to anticipate the order of events, so try playing 'this little piggy' or singing 'round and round the garden, like a teddy bear, one step, two step, tickly under there'. You'll see her gradually starting to realize that she's about to be tickled, and giggling in anticipation.

WHEN TO WORRY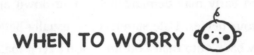

If your baby isn't sitting unsupported by now, have a chat with your doctor or health visitor, as sometimes this can indicate a developmental problem or a condition such as cerebral palsy.

Likewise, speak to a health professional if your baby isn't yet grasping or grabbing – again, there's a slight chance this could be due to cerebral palsy, or perhaps a vision problem.

SAFETY TIP OF THE MONTH

Beware of small objects

Your baby will be putting lots of things in her mouth at the moment. This phase begins from as early as 6 months, but peaks around now and becomes especially problematic once your baby is crawling and on the move, popping interesting objects into her mouth as she goes.

You'll soon be picking up loose change and pen tops automatically, and you'll continue doing this until your baby is about 13 months old, when mouthing everything becomes much less of an issue. And by the time she is 3 years of age you'll hardly have to worry at all because most toys with small parts are recommended for children aged 3 and upwards. But do be aware that children can and do choke later than this.

WHEN TO SEE THE DOCTOR ✚

Coeliac Disease

This condition basically means intolerance to gluten and can occur several months after your baby has started to eat gluten – which is found in wheat, rye and barley. So bread, biscuits, cakes and many processed foods can cause problems. Eating gluten actually causes damage to the lining of the small intestine, which means the body can't absorb nutrients properly.

Symptoms include frequent, smelly poos that are a greyish colour, a swollen tummy, and being extremely miserable – undiagnosed coeliac babies are hungry and very, very unhappy. If the condition isn't picked up quickly, your baby could end up not gaining enough weight and have slow bone growth.

Coeliac disease is more common in babies of Celtic origin – typically those with blue eyes and blonde hair.

If you are concerned, your doctor may do a blood test. But if your doctor doesn't think your baby has coeliac disease, he is almost certainly right, as it is extremely rare. By all means ask for a second opinion, because it's important to put your mind at rest, but we'd put money on you getting the same answer from another doctor.

There are so many things that can cause babies of this age to be miserable – teething and a cold being the most likely.

If your baby does have coeliac disease, she will have to stick to a gluten-free diet for life, but you will be given full advice and information from a dietician. And there are plenty of gluten-free products available, including breads, cakes and biscuits. Your baby's symptoms should improve within about 2 weeks of going on such a diet.

WHAT'S HAPPENING TO MUM AND DAD

Some mums will be pregnant again by now, and if this includes you, then congratulations – it will be wonderful for your baby to have a sibling so close in age. Or perhaps you're thinking about another baby and wondering when the right time is.

The advantages of a closely spaced family are numerous. First, your eldest won't suffer too much from jealousy because she'll still be a baby herself; also you get the slog of being pregnant and having very young children over and done with. If you work, then your maternity leave for the new baby will also give you extra time to spend with your toddler, your children will be close in age and have lots in common so will play well together and with each others' toys, and you'll still have all your old baby stuff to recycle for baby number two. Finally, ideas and theories on bringing up babies won't have changed much, your children will have similar routines and needs, and you won't have forgotten how to look after a new baby.

But spacing your family gives you plenty of advantages, too. For example, your body will have had more time to recover and you'll feel that you've got your energy back, your eldest will be more grown up and easier to look after and may even be able to help a little with your new baby, and the new baby stage will seem more exciting if it's been a while since you've done it. A bigger age gap between children can mean that they squabble a little less, although this isn't always the case. You won't need a double buggy, you won't have two babies in nappies, and in many ways it's not as much hard work.

Whatever you and your partner decide, you'll have the experience of knowing how to look after a baby; this is a huge benefit – most mums agree that subsequent babies tend to be easier because they have to fit around the family and so are more laid back.

PLANNING AHEAD

If you need to leave your baby with a carer, perhaps you're going back to work or you want to start using a babysitter, allow time for your baby to bond with her carer before being left. This is important now that she's at the age for separation anxiety to be an issue.

Likewise with grandparents – allow time for your baby to get used to them if she's not seen them for a while, especially if you're planning to leave them to babysit.

It's also worth booking doctor and dental appointments for yourself around now, because you're entitled to free dental care and prescriptions while your child is under one. So getting organized could save you some money.

MONTH 10

INTRODUCTION

This month you'll need to be aware of separation anxiety, better known as stranger phobia or simply 'clinginess'. This will soon peak, and particularly affects babies aged 12 to 18 months.

Instead of flirting with the entire world, your baby may now start to cling to you if there are strangers around. She may become upset if you leave the room, and could well howl mournfully if you disappear to use the toilet.

Although this stage is a bit tedious, separation anxiety is a normal developmental stage and a sign that your baby is maturing emotionally. The response is actually triggered in the lower, primitive part of the brain, and your baby will feel genuinely distressed – it's a primeval safety mechanism that ensures a mother doesn't leave or forget a vulnerable baby. In caveman times it could mean the difference between life and death.

So don't be in a hurry to make your baby grow up – allow her to follow you around and, if she wants to cling to you, let her if possible. It's a normal stage of growing up and you won't do any harm whatsoever in 'babying' your baby. In fact, paediatricians and other health professionals can be concerned if there are no signs of separation anxiety, if, say, a child is left with a stranger, because this can indicate a lack of bonding with the mother.

Some babies are naturally more outgoing so will be less clingy, as will those who have had lots of carers – but all babies should show separation anxiety to some extent.

Separation anxiety gradually decreases as the 'thinking' part of your baby's brain matures and inhibits her primitive responses so she'll no longer feel desperately upset when Mum has to go. Things usually improve by the age of 2, although lots of children still struggle from time to time with separation anxiety up to the age of about 5. By this age a child will have the language capability to communicate her emotional needs: 'Mummy, I don't want you to go, will you be coming back soon?' And of course she will get the reassurance she needs.

Do warn friends and family who don't see your baby regularly not to be offended if they dive in and pick her up and she screams with fear. Well-meaning family – grandparents, uncles and aunts – can sometimes feel upset if a baby doesn't return their affection.

Thankfully, your baby is able to attach herself to other main carers in her life, not just you. So if you're going back to work and need childcare, she'll form a bond with the person who's looking after her.

Ensure that your baby's carer is emotionally intelligent and takes time to comfort and soothe her with lots of cuddles when you leave. And do allow time for your baby to become used to her new carer. Perhaps stay with your baby the first time they meet, leaving the room for about 10 minutes, then on another occasion extending this to 30 minutes, then a little longer. Once a strong bond has been formed, she'll cope much better with being left.

SLEEP

Aim: uninterrupted night sleep 9–12 hours
To bed early – about 7 or 8 p.m.
One or two naps: *sometimes a short (20- to 30-minute) morning nap, plus a longer lunchtime nap (2–3 hours)*
A total of 14½ hours' sleep

This is a good month to lower your baby's cot mattress, because if she's not standing yet she soon will be – and you don't want her vaulting out! This usually involves just relocating some retaining bolts around the cot, but check your cot's instruction manual for details.

This is also the time when some babies start to need a special toy or blanket that they like to sleep with. It's worth encouraging this, as it can help your baby sleep well at night – she'll find comfort in her toy rather than needing you whenever she wakes. This will be particularly useful once separation anxiety starts to affect her sleep – usually from around Month 15, when some babies start to protest if you leave the room at night, and also wake in the night and worry because you're not there.

We talk more about comfort toys and separation anxiety in Month 15.

Head-banging

Some babies will start head-banging at around this age – rhythmically bumping their heads against their cots as a way of soothing themselves and getting to sleep, because rhythm is calming to babies. Likewise sucking on a dummy is very rhythmic, and similarly tugging on a comfort blanket is soothing before sleep.

Head-banging is quite common, affecting up to one in five children, and is three times more likely in boys. If your child does this, there's little you can do apart from wait it out, as this phase generally stops by the time your child is 2. It usually starts by the time your child is 1.

Although head-banging is alarming to watch, it's rarely anything to worry about. Your child won't do herself any harm and, even in the case of severe head-bangers, scans have shown no evidence of damage.

So don't be tempted to rush in and pick your child up when she's banging her head, or she'll end up with bad sleeping habits – she'll come to rely on you for comfort to get to sleep instead of her own (rather strange) self-soothing method. Try to be thankful that your child is able to get to sleep by herself – lots of children can't.

Sometimes rhythmic banging is associated with autism, learning difficulties and some forms of epilepsy, but if your child has a developmental problem you will probably already know about it because there will be plenty of other behavioural warning signs.

It's also worth flagging up to your doctor if your child seems to be in any pain or discomfort, because sometimes babies head-bang if they have an ear infection or even something in their ear.

Troubleshooting

My baby has started standing up in her cot and won't go to sleep
Once your baby can stand, she'll be so delighted by her new skill that she'll practise at every opportunity, including in her cot. This is an ideal place because it has bars to help her pull up, and also a soft mattress to land on. So she'll end up feeling excited and not sleepy.

Continue with your usual routine of kissing her goodnight and then leaving the room, giving her all the usual cues that it's time to sleep. Let her stand if she wants to – you can't stop her. She'll probably become bored and tired after a while, then lie down and go to sleep.

Do note that lots of early standers have an added problem in that they find it difficult to sit down again, so will cry out for help. If this is the case, help your baby to lie down, say goodnight in the usual way and leave the room. In a couple of weeks she'll not only have learned how to sit down again by herself, but she won't be so obsessed with wanting to stand in the first place, which will mean she'll settle more easily.

Your baby may also wake in the night and stand up – but this phase will be even shorter than standing up at bedtime, because she'll be tired. The key is not to make a fuss but simply allow your baby to enjoy a week or two of standing practice before she gets bored.

The upside is that your baby may have fun standing up in the morning and so not cry for you quite so soon after waking.

Cleaning my baby's teeth upsets her bedtime routine

Every evening you may give your baby a calming bath and a soothing massage followed by warm milk. Then it's time to clean her teeth and she becomes extremely agitated and wide awake as she tries to wriggle away from the brush.

This is very common and most babies don't cooperate with teeth-cleaning before the age of about 2. We suggest that you back off and don't worry too much about diligent brushing, because the key to preventing tooth decay in babies isn't brushing but diet (see below: A Tooth-friendly Diet).

You can try wiping your baby's front teeth with a damp cloth or cotton bud. When her back teeth (molars) come through, you can try brushing very gently. She may open her mouth if you give her a brush to hold herself, and then you can brush with a second brush – do use infant brushes which are small and soft. You can also try cleaning your own teeth, then letting your baby copy.

At best you'll be able to brush for a few seconds most nights – sometimes she simply won't let you brush at all. But at this stage it's more about teaching the tooth-brushing habit than actual cleaning.

A Tooth-friendly Diet

Avoid sugary foods such as biscuits and jams. Don't allow your baby to drink squashes or fruit juices – even diluted pure fruit juices are harmful. As for milk, your baby obviously needs it but, as we've said before, do ensure that she doesn't fall asleep with a bottle because she'll have a pool of milk around her teeth, which can cause decay. Water is the most tooth-friendly drink.

See Month 22 for more on a tooth-friendly diet.

FEEDING

Around now, spoon-fed babies sometimes clamp their mouths shut and turn their heads away – a clear indication that they don't want to eat. It really doesn't matter if your baby misses the odd meal, or indeed goes for a couple of days without eating much. Just check that she doesn't become dehydrated (i.e. if her nappy remains dry for longer than a couple of hours).

Rather than trying to force your baby to eat, force yourself to relax, because she really will become hungry again before too long.

Five Reasons Babies Refuse Food

1. **You've been forcing her** – overenthusiastic spoon-feeding is very common and can put babies right off their food. Food is one of the few things your baby has a lot of control over, and she may be sending a very clear message that she's not happy with the situation. So let her try feeding herself, or just playing with her food.

2. **She's full** – babies often have a few mouthfuls, then stop eating. Even if your baby doesn't eat as much as usual, she may have had enough. Try to let her be the judge of how much food she needs.

3. **She's full of milk** – your baby should be having about a pint of formula or breastmilk a day by now – that's about two to three feeds. If she has much more it will affect her appetite. See next month's section on Feeding (page 86).

4. **She's tired, ill or teething** – these can all put your baby off eating. Try giving her something plain and soft, such as a ripe banana – we all have days when we can't face rich food. She may want more milk than usual – comfort-sucking will help her cope

with any pain. This is fine for a day or two, but take care not to allow your baby to get into the habit of filling up on milk and not eating enough solids.

5. **She's bored** – your baby may be fed up with what you're giving her, or some babies are naturally less interested in food than others. Give her finger food, because then there's always something to 'play' with. She could also have her own spoon. Some babies at this age cooperate better with being spoon-fed if they have something in their hands to keep them occupied. And let your baby share the family meal – babies love mimicking, and will be curious to eat what you're having.

DEVELOPMENT AND PLAY

Talking and Communicating

Your baby's understanding continues to develop, and if you ask 'Where's Daddy?' or 'Where's your coat?' she may point or even go and look. Your baby may be able to nod and shake her head this month to express 'yes' and 'no,' especially if you ask her questions. So you can try asking her if she wants a bath toy, or more food.

If your baby is an early talker, she will continue to form the beginnings of words this month – at first you won't be sure if it's just coincidence or if she's really trying to utter actual words.

Talking takes a lot of concentration, so you'll find that your baby goes for hours hardly 'saying' anything at all, and then has a period of being very noisy. This is normal and there's no point trying to *make* your baby 'talk'.

Try to chatter away to your baby throughout the day, and repeat words so that she gradually learns them – for example, 'Let's go and find your coat, here's your coat, let's put your coat on, let's do your coat up.' You may well find that you're doing this anyway without thinking.

Interestingly, at between 10 and 12 months old your baby will begin to lose her ability to hear all sounds in different languages; she's now starting to specialize in her native tongue.

Understands 'No'
By 10 months babies can pick up on intonation and will start to realize that a sharp tone means 'Stop' or 'No.'

Babies differ in how much notice they take when you warn them – for instance not to play with a plug socket – some will stop immediately, others will simply carry on.

You obviously can't discipline a baby of this age – she's not trying to annoy you in any way, she's just incredibly curious about the world. All you can really do is to repeat your 'No' and give a reason: 'Electricity can hurt you.' Your baby won't understand every word, but giving an explanation keeps your voice calm and authoritative.

Then pick your baby up and get her interested in something else – it's easy to distract babies of this age. But most importantly, keep baby-proofing your home so that there's not too much that she's 'not allowed' to do. (More on saying 'No' in Month 15.)

MILESTONES

(All babies are different – you probably won't be able to tick everything on this list.)

☐ *Cruising* – some babies will not only be standing up this month, but will be using furniture to balance as they shuffle around sideways. It can be tempting to try to speed up your baby's walking progress by standing behind her and holding her hands, but she will wobble around like a tree in a storm with no balance or stability. This is a very unnatural way for her to walk. Babies actually learn to walk leaning forwards – a bit like apes. So get down

Babies learn to walk leaning forwards, so encourage her to use a pushcart.

on your knees and hold her hands from the front. Or give her a pushcart to balance on. Do bear in mind that giving your baby walking practice means that she may start demanding that you help her to walk as a fun game, and get quite irritated if you don't cooperate immediately. So if she's not yet able to use a pushcart to walk, it's probably better to leave walking practice for a little while.

☐ *Crawling down the stairs* – if your baby has started trying to crawl, she will have the motor skills to climb down the stairs from this month – the sooner she learns this, the safer she will be. She should climb down backwards, feet first. You will have to spend a lot of time teaching her – a couple of times a day for at least a week. Your baby will think it's great fun if Mum or Dad starts to climb down the stairs with her, and more importantly, once she is competent at crawling down the stairs she won't fall. We can't recommend this highly enough, because babies frequently fall down the stairs, even in houses with stair gates – these can be accidently left open or pushed over. As well as teaching your baby to climb down the stairs, you can teach her to crawl *up* – she'll find this much easier because she can see where she's going.

☐ *Advanced crawling* – even babies who are starting to cruise will rely on crawling when they want to get somewhere in a hurry – babies learn to crawl at a very quick pace and to turn around while crawling.

☐ *Dropping things* – some babies start to drop things out of their buggies and highchairs this month. So watch out that you don't lose baby cups and bottles when you're out with the buggy. You can try toys that strap onto the front bar of the buggy so that you don't lose them. Please note that dropping things is different from 'casting out', which occurs from next month and is when babies learn to throw.

☐ *Using hands independently* – at around this time you can pass your baby a small brick, then when you pass her another brick she'll be able to take it in her other hand – she may even bang the bricks together. Up until now she wouldn't have been able to use both hands for different tasks, but would have dropped the first brick before taking the second one.

☐ *Clapping* – some babies will be able to clap around now if you show them how. And even if your baby can't clap just yet, she'll enjoy the sound of other people clapping.

☐ *Waving* – she may understand 'Bye-bye' and 'Hello' this month, and may start to wave her arm, especially if you take a little time to teach her.

☐ *Jealousy* – from about this age your baby may become upset if she sees you picking up another baby, or perhaps giving attention to an older sibling. It may appear that she's jealous and being manipulative in trying to get your attention, but in fact this response is linked with separation anxiety. She's genuinely concerned that her main 'carer' isn't available to look after her. It's always difficult with more than one child, but gently reassure her – 'Don't worry, I'm still here, would you like a cuddle?'

☐ *Sitting on Dad's shoulders* – your baby will be able to support herself well enough now to enjoy this. Dad should keep a tight hold of her legs, though.

☐ *Starts to like baby medicine* – you may be familiar with the battle of getting your baby to take medicines such as Calpol or other liquid infant painkillers. But from around this age most babies will start to enjoy the sweet, child-friendly flavours, and actually like having medicine.

WHEN TO WORRY

We suggested a few simple eye checks in month 6. You can check your baby's eyes again now, and if you notice any of the following, see your doctor:

- Your baby doesn't follow a small object up and down and from side to side, or she seems to move her head instead of her eyes.
- She seems to hold her head at an odd angle in order to look at an object – you're likely to notice this once she's sitting up.
- Her eyelids are different levels because one of them is droopy – again, you'll notice this once she's sitting up. This is called a *ptosis*, and if the eyelid droops partially over the pupil it can stop light from entering the eye and, potentially, reduce vision. Often an ophthalmologist will simply monitor the condition, but occasionally surgery is needed to lift the lid and allow light to enter the eye to ensure that vision develops normally.

It's also worth seeing your health visitor if your baby won't eat lumpy purees or finger foods. Some babies get stuck on smooth purees and refuse to eat anything else, so may need a referral to a paediatric dietician.

SAFETY TIP OF THE MONTH

You've probably taken measures to baby-proof your home already, perhaps using plug-socket covers, cupboard locks, corner covers and stair gates. Now that your baby is standing, or soon-to-be standing, you need to think beyond floor level. So watch out for curtain and blind cords, which are a potential strangling risk – get into the habit of tying them up out of reach (you'll need to fix a hook to the wall, up high). Or you can buy a cord-winder from Mothercare, to wind the cord and keep it out of reach of your child.

You should also get into the habit of using the back of the cooker hob and keeping saucepan handles turned to the back. Also make sure that knives and hot cups of tea aren't left on the edge of tables, because it won't be long before your baby is standing up and reaching for objects on high surfaces.

WHEN TO SEE THE DOCTOR

Urinary Tract Infection (UTI)

If you notice fishy-smelling wee when you change your baby's nappy, it's worth being aware of UTIs. There is usually a fever, temperature above 38°C, vomiting and sometimes pain on urination with this condition. You may also notice that your baby wees more frequently, and only does a little bit of wee – of course this pattern is difficult to spot when your baby is in nappies, but over the coming months your baby will go longer without weeing in her nappy, which makes such a pattern easier to detect.

It's important to see a doctor quickly, who will do a urine test and prescribe antibiotics if it is positive. Your doctor may refer your baby to hospital to check for kidney damage.

A urinary tract infection is 10 times more likely to affect girls than boys because they have a shorter urethra (the tube that leads from the bladder to the outside of the body), so it's easier for bacteria to enter the body. This is why it's important to wipe girls from front to back when changing their nappies, to prevent bacteria crossing from the bowel to the bladder.

Boy babies with a UTI ring more alarm bells because they are less prone to these, so it is more likely to be a sign of kidney problems, although this is still very unlikely.

WHAT'S HAPPENING TO MUM AND DAD

You may be taking maximum maternity leave – 12 months – in which case you'll be due back to work at the end of next month. As well as the emotional aspect of spending long periods of time away from your baby, do think about some of the practicalities.

First, when you're on maternity leave you build up holiday entitlement, so if you return to work in, say, June, you'll be entitled to take a whole year's worth of holiday between June and December. Do note that most employers don't allow you to carry over holiday from one year to the next, so if you return to work in January, you won't have any holiday leave from the previous year.

Another thing to think about is flexible working. Parents of children under 6 are entitled to put in a request for this, and by law your employer has to give it consideration. Both you and your partner are entitled to this, so perhaps you could sit down together and plan the ideal working plan for your new family, then see if your employers will approve it.

Here are some flexible work options to consider. Part-time is the obvious one. For Mum this would reduce your maternity payments for any future maternity leaves, however, so you might be better off going part-time once you've completed your family.

You could also request a day or two a week working from home – don't tell your employers that it's because you want to spend more time with your baby, because they'll worry that you won't be doing enough work. Make it clear that you have childcare arrangements for when you're working from home but that the arrangement would cut down on the cost of childcare because you're not paying for commuting time. Suggest a work plan to your employers, demonstrating which tasks you could easily do from home.

Another option is to work a five-day week in four days, i.e. four very long days. Again, this can cut down on childcare costs, and also gives you an extra day with your baby. But of course it will be tough on the days when you've been up all night with your baby but have to stay very late at work.

You could also suggest that you start very early on one or two days, and leave early – this will give you time with your baby at the end of the day.

Whatever your request, your employers must have a meeting with you within 28 days of receiving your application to talk about your request, then they have to give you a written response within 14 days. If they say no, you have 14 days to appeal their decision.

PLANNING AHEAD

If you're going back to work at the end of next month and want to request flexible working, try to get your application in soon, because you'll have to wait up to 28 days for an initial response and meeting.

It's also worth trying on your work clothes and shoes – lots of women don't manage to lose all their baby weight in the first year, so you might need to go shopping.

You could ask your employer if you can go in for a couple of 'keeping in touch' days before you're back full-time. You're entitled to 10 of these while you're on maternity leave, and it will make your first proper day back at work less nerve-wracking. More important, it will give you and your baby a chance to try out new childcare arrangements.

MONTH 11

INTRODUCTION

It's a strange phenomenon, but most children stop seeming so much like 'babies' this month and start to become more toddler-like. Something about their facial expressions, posture and mannerisms changes around now. Instead of grinning happily at everyone and everything, your baby will be more curious and have a more intent expression. When she looks at you, it will be with less unconditional delight but with more connection and understanding of what she sees.

And now, when you hold your baby, she won't melt into your form the way she used to, but will be stronger, more upright and able to support her own weight and look around the room.

She'll also be starting to show attitude if she doesn't like something – if she doesn't want to go in her buggy, she won't cry in an upset way but will get quite cross and cry in a 'shouty' way. (See Milestones, page 89, for more on attitude.)

Your baby's emerging personality is nothing to worry about – it's normal for babies to start wanting their own way from time to time. There's no need even to think about punishment at this age. Attitude in babies is not a sign that they will grow up spoilt and overindulged, despite all the newspaper stories about pampered children and 'soft' parents. Your child is still very much a baby, and it's far too soon to start trying to teach her 'good behaviour'. At this stage it's more a case of managing her behaviour and knowing a few tricks so that you can, for example, get her into the car seat quickly even if she's protesting. After that you can gradually introduce discipline, keeping it age-appropriate. We shall be returning to this subject in coming months.

This is also the month of food-throwing – an important developmental stage. Again, there's no point getting cross with your baby, as this is normal behaviour – just have a roll of kitchen towel and a dustpan and brush handy. Some mums put a mat down under the highchair; others rely on the family dog to clear up …

SLEEP

Aim: uninterrupted night sleep 10–12 hours
To bed early – about 7 or 8 p.m.
One or two naps: sometimes a short (20- to 30-minute) morning nap, plus a longer lunchtime nap (2–3 hours)
A total of 14½ hours' sleep

It's known that babies can become more set in their ways once they are 12 months old. You may already be noticing signs of attitude setting in, and your baby is going to become gradually more stubborn and determined from now on. So this month is a good time to give sleep-training a really good try and get your baby out of any bad habits, because the longer you leave it, the harder it will get.

There's nothing like a deadline to improve a baby's sleep habits, and working mums often put in a lot of time sleep-training their baby before they go back to work – and they nearly always get good results.

The bottom line is, teaching your baby to sleep well takes time and energy, and it can be exhausting. So if you've been postponing getting rid of the dummy, stopping the final night-feed or sorting out bedtime fussing, then now's a good time to tackle it before your baby gets too set in her ways. You can follow the various sleep-training techniques and tips we have given over the last few months.

As for getting rid of your baby's dummy, there really isn't a nice or easy way of doing this because your baby will get upset. We've found that going cold turkey works best – you check that your baby isn't ill or teething, then throw all dummies away. When your baby cries for her dummy, you can look her in the eye and say, 'It's gone,' and really mean it. If you've hidden it 'just in case', you'll be tempted to get it out in the middle of the night. Your baby will have about three very distraught nights, then gradually get used to sleeping without her dummy, and probably won't even ask for it after a week. We really don't believe there is a gentle way of doing this.

The only compromise we can think of is to allow your baby to have her dummy at night but ban it during the day – this is because she's about to start talking and dummies can hinder speech development.

Troubleshooting

My baby sleeps better on her front
It's true that some babies seem to sleep better on their tummies, but because of the cot death risk parents shouldn't put them down on their fronts to sleep. However, by now your baby is probably rolling easily both ways, and may well roll over onto her side or front from time to time while she's asleep – there's no need to put her onto her back again if she does this.

At bedtime you could put her into her cot sitting up (assuming she's been sitting a couple of months and is a strong sitter), then let her choose her sleeping position. This is a great sleeping skill for babies to learn, although it may take a little longer for her to get to sleep than previously. The big advantage is that your baby may transfer her new skill to the mornings – which is fantastic if she's an early riser, sits up for a while, then chooses to get into her sleeping position and go back to sleep.

FEEDING

If you've been letting your baby have her own spoon, she'll be making some progress by now, although she'll be making plenty of mess, too. Interestingly, babies in large families often learn to feed themselves earlier because they get fed up with waiting for Mum to spoon them their food. So you can try giving your baby a spoon and letting her get on with it. There may well be times when you'll also want to use a separate spoon to help feed your baby, just to speed things along a bit. Or perhaps just load her spoon for her.

You could also try letting your baby have a go at drinking out of a cup with no lid – give her just a centimetre of water at first, because she is bound to spill it.

Too Much Milk at Night

Last month we explored different reasons why babies sometimes refuse to eat. Probably the most difficult of these to tackle is if she's still drinking too much milk, particularly at night.

As we mentioned in Month 6, it's important to stop night-feeding because this helps build your baby's daytime appetite. Some babies, particularly bed-sharers and breastfeeders, drink throughout the night and eat hardly anything during the day.

This can happen if mothers are particularly exhausted – maybe they have more than one child or they get very little support. They are in survival mode – desperate for some sleep at night, they allow their baby to feed because they haven't got the energy to resist.

Other mothers enjoy cuddling and nurturing their babies so much that they find it difficult to cut down on breastfeeding – without realizing it, they may be trying to hang on to the baby-stage for too long.

It's important to break this pattern now that your baby is old enough to be eating three solid meals a day, or she could end up with feeding problems. The answer sounds simple: you stop feeding your baby at night. This is easier said than done, though, because she'll cry, you'll probably cry, and it will be hellish. You can cuddle her and offer her water, although this won't help much if she's desperate for milk. Hang on in there, because by the morning she'll be ravenous and the night-feeding pattern will begin to break. Give her a proper breakfast rather than breastfeed – she'll eat well, then you can breastfeed her after breakfast. She won't want as much milk as usual, so you may have to express a little.

This will have been a very tough night for you both, but sometimes you do have to be cruel to be kind. It will take a few nights to turn things around completely, but your baby will feed better in the day, sleep better at night and be happier. You'll be happier, too, because your nights won't be broken and you won't be worrying about your baby not eating properly.

Lots of mums get themselves into this situation of giving their baby too much milk, and plenty of them go to a feeding clinic for support. So don't hesitate to get a referral from your GP, because it's a problem that can be quickly solved.

DEVELOPMENT AND PLAY

Talking

Your baby may start to copy you when you speak by using her own language and mimicking the rhythm of your words. This is called 'jargoning' and you'll hear your baby chattering away as she pretends to talk.

We've mentioned animal noises in Month 9, and by now some babies will be very good at imitating anything from the quack of the ducks in the park to the clicking of the indicators in the car – do encourage this with lots of praise, because making different sounds will help speech development. And if your baby isn't yet making animal noises, she'll enjoy listening to them and this is a fun way to teach her the names of animals. She'll understand even if she doesn't yet join in.

If your baby's an early talker she may say a couple of words this month – she may not say them perfectly – 'nana' may mean 'banana' – but you will both know exactly what she means.

MILESTONES

(All babies are different – you probably won't be able to tick everything on this list.)

☐ *Experimenting* – your baby probably understands cause and effect by now, and will have great fun experimenting, perhaps by pushing a toy under the bath water and watching it bob up. Or if you blow bubbles for her, she'll enjoy popping them.

☐ *Mimicking* – your baby may copy your facial expressions as she watches you this month. This is different to the early months when she may have mimicked you sticking your tongue out – now she is able to copy more detailed expressions such as frowns or the way you smile and laugh. She will continue to do this well into her third year.

☐ *Pulling hair* – babies often yank long hair around now, if they haven't done so already. She isn't trying to hurt, even though she has the strength to yank quite hard. She simply has the coordination and control to be able to grab at fascinating-looking hair that is irresistible to touch. You can try teaching her, 'No, that hurts' and perhaps show her how to stroke hair gently. But it's probably easier to tie your hair back and warn friends and family members who have long hair.

☐ *Humour* – you can start to make very simple jokes from around now and your baby will actually laugh. For example, throwing a ball in the air and 'accidentally' dropping it and pretending to be surprised.

☐ *Starts to resist* – some babies develop attitude around now and may protest when it's time to get in the buggy, be strapped in the car or get dressed. It can be a bit of a surprise when your once placid little bundle starts to resist, but this is normal behaviour because she is learning to assert herself as an individual. You could try distraction – 'Ooh, look at that big lorry over there' while you quickly strap her into her buggy. But we recommend that you calmly explain that she doesn't have a choice, then firmly pick her up and put her in. You'll find that once your baby is strapped in, she stops protesting pretty quickly. This is why we think decisive, quick action is better than patient coaxing in these circumstances. Do note that mothers with more than one child barely notice this phase – they just get on and put the youngest into her buggy however much fuss she's making – after all, they're used to their older children being able to resist with a lot more force and strength than a baby!

☐ *Throwing* – your baby will already know how to drop things. Now she's old enough to start throwing. Some babies will have great fun chucking lumps of banana, cups, plates, toys, pots of nappy cream and anything they can get their hands on. If your baby is going to be a chucker, she'll lob things from her buggy, highchair and cot, and will delight in watching things hurtling across the room. This is a normal developmental stage, known as 'casting out', and while it can be annoying if your baby hurls her lunch across the kitchen, rest assured that she'll soon tire of throwing everything, especially if you don't give her a big reaction by getting cross.

WHEN TO WORRY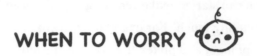

If your baby still isn't babbling, or doesn't look at you when you talk to her, it is worth mentioning to your doctor or health visitor, especially if she doesn't seem interested in trying to communicate with you. It's possible that your baby has a hearing problem.

If your baby hates loud noises and is very sensitive to noise, this can also indicate a hearing problem. Watch out for her putting her hands over her ears when she hears a loud noise.

SAFETY TIP OF THE MONTH (i)

Unexpected night awakenings

If your baby wakes up in the night you will be more likely to ignore her or leave her to resettle herself than when she was very young. But it's important that you don't ignore your baby if she is ill and has a fever – you'll need to give her Calpol or baby ibuprofen to bring her temperature down. So if she wakes unexpectedly and doesn't settle quite quickly, check her temperature to ensure she doesn't have a fever.

WHEN TO SEE THE DOCTOR

Teething

Teething can be prolonged and painful, and your baby may seem quite miserable when she's going through it. But it's important not to mistake a more serious condition for teething, especially if you've witnessed a few teeth coming through and are familiar with the symptoms.

Here's how to spot teething and how to spot other ailments with similar symptoms.

First, do be aware of the side effects of teething. The pain can cause irritability, clinginess, crying, disturbed sleep and ear-rubbing. Other symptoms include biting, red gums, red cheeks and excessive dribbling which can irritate the skin around the mouth and chin (dab your baby's chin gently, because rubbing triggers more saliva production). You can also use aqueous cream (available from pharmacies). The extra saliva is also thought to loosen the bowels because it over-digests your baby's food.

Here are some teething symptoms that can mask more serious ailments:

- Pain – although your baby can't verbalize that she's in pain, if you suspect teething then do give her pain-relief medicine such as Calpol – if you're right she will cheer up within about 25 minutes. Anaesthetic gels such as Bonjela and cooled teething rings can also give relief. Teething doesn't cause a fever, so before giving pain-relief medicine, check your baby's temperature (it should be below 38°C). If your baby has a fever, then the cause of her pain is illness, not teething, so you need to work out what is wrong. At this age it could well be a viral upper respiratory tract infection. You can still give her pain relief, as this will help bring her temperature down. You can give both baby paracetamol (Calpol) and baby ibuprofen together for extra-strong pain relief (see Month 23).
- Diarrhoea – loose stools are common when teething, but take care not to overlook a genuine case of diarrhoea. So look out for stools that are explosive, particularly smelly, watery or bloody – then keep her fluids topped up and take her to the doctor if she doesn't improve within 24 hours. And if she has a fever, this is a clear sign she has genuine diarrhoea caused by infection, so take her to the doctor.

- Ear-rubbing – ear-rubbing and -pulling are a common teething symptom, but babies also do this if they have an ear infection. With an infection your baby may also be doing high-pitched crying or have a cold. Take your baby to the doctor if pain-relief medicine doesn't help, if she has a fever, or if she doesn't seem better after a couple of days.

Alternatives

If you would like to try an alternative remedy to treat teething, then lots of mums swear by homoeopathic teething granules which you can dab on your baby's tongue. And some parents give their babies amber teething necklaces to wear – amber is known for its healing and calming properties.

If these don't seem to work for your child, though, don't hold back on the Calpol or baby ibuprofen, both of which are clinically proven to relieve pain.

WHAT'S HAPPENING TO MUM AND DAD

Your baby's first birthday is coming up at the end of this month and it's a wonderful milestone. You and your partner may decide to have a party to celebrate.

If money is tight, you can get away with a low-budget party with just a few close friends and family – there's no need to invite baby-friends for your 1-year-old, as she's too young to appreciate company her own age.

To keep the cost down you can buy a pack of children's party invitations, because these always have a section for the 'time' which you can fill in, say from 3–5 p.m. People generally don't go mad on the alcohol at this time, and most opt for cups of tea or coffee. You could offer traditional children's party food such as tiny cheese and marmite sandwiches, mini-sausages, jammy dodgers and jelly and ice cream – and of course a birthday cake. It will all seem charmingly retro and your baby will love tucking into her birthday feast – even 1-year-olds are allowed to be a little unhealthy on their birthday.

PLANNING AHEAD

Here are some birthday present suggestions that will give plenty of play value for the coming year and longer.

First, a sturdy push-along toy can help your baby to balance. She'll use it to help get onto her feet and to walk along in the correct postural walking position. With time she may put things into the cart, such as bricks.

You could also buy a ride-on toy which, again, she'll use to help get to her feet – make sure that it's small enough for her to climb on (she'll be able to do this in a few months if she can't now) and sturdy enough not to tip over easily. Choose something with a storage section which she will love putting small toys into.

Your baby will also love toys with little people and figures that she can play with, such as a bus, car, or house – she'll have fun 'posting' the people through doors and organizing them, and perhaps even talking to them.

A ball also makes a good present for this age – your baby can play with a ball while she's still crawling by rolling it across a room, and of course one day she will be able to kick and throw it.

And don't forget bricks, which will have play value for years and years.

MONTH 12

INTRODUCTION

So you've hit the amazing milestone of 12 months. Your once tiny newborn is now a year old and may well be starting to walk or talk. She will babble away, play with toys, feed herself and even have opinions about what she does or doesn't want.

The coming year is tremendously exciting and one in which your baby will learn vast amounts. By her second birthday she'll be chatting, running, climbing and even arguing (using two- and three-word sentences).

We hope you enjoy every moment of these incredible developmental milestones, because there won't be another year quite like it, and there's something rather special about 1-year-olds. They're still baby-shaped and cuddly, with their big tummies and short limbs, but now they are their own person and grow more independent by the day.

Most don't say a great deal and will go for long spells being completely mute, and yet they will understand a lot of what's going on – more than most parents realize. Some 1-year-olds will carry on crawling until they are 18 months old, oblivious to the fact that babies 6 months younger than them are already walking. And when they do start walking it will be a wobbly toddle – you'll soon see how the term 'toddler' came about.

Although your 1-year-old will look like a giant when you put her next to a newborn, we urge you to still think of her as a baby, as this will help you to remain gentle and patient and not expect too much. Just as she would have pushed your patience when she was a newborn by wanting to feed every few hours day and night, she'll continue to challenge you as her personality comes through and she starts to want things her own way. She'll demand more attention than ever and it will seem as though she's always busy, often putting herself in danger, and so will need constant watching – this can be exhausting but it's actually very normal. And she will eventually need less watching, usually from about the age of 2.

Shortly after her first birthday, your baby will be due for her meningitis C and Hib booster. Your baby is far more aware of what's going on than when she had her last immunization at 4 months, so we suggest telling her in advance what's going to happen. She won't understand the details but she'll probably understand that something is going to happen; just reassure her that it will be OK. Before you go to the doctor's, explain that she's going to have a little prick in her leg (show her where, i.e. on her thigh). And tell your baby it will hurt a bit – like the time when she 'had a splinter', 'fell over' and so on. Then say that the doctor will put a plaster on and it will all be better again.

Distraction has been shown to help children through medical procedures, which is why hospital play therapists use distraction techniques routinely. So when your baby has her vaccination, you could take a new toy along with you – something cheap from a newsagent should do the trick as long as your child hasn't seen it before. Then give it to your child just before the needle goes in.

SLEEP

Aim: uninterrupted night sleep 10–12 hours
To bed early – about 7 or 8 p.m.
One or two naps: sometimes a short (20- to 30-minute) morning nap, plus a
longer lunchtime nap (2–3 hours)
A total of 14½ hours' sleep

Some experts say you can let your baby use a pillow from the age of 1. Your baby doesn't actually need one, though, so you may want to wait until she is older. If you do decide to get her a pillow, choose a very flat one, or a toddler pillow – she's too small for anything too big and fluffy.

Some parents find that a pillow seems to improve their toddler's sleep. It makes going to bed seem grown up and fun for a few nights – they love copying Mummy and Daddy. And perhaps a pillow makes sleeping on her side more comfortable. Also, having her head propped up slightly can ease the symptoms of a cold because she'll get less bunged up.

Troubleshooting

My baby's sleeping bag restricts her when she tries to stand in her cot
Baby sleeping bags are a great invention – your baby can be warm and snug and never kick her blankets off. But when your baby is old enough to stand up, a sleeping bag will get in her way and possibly annoy her.

It can be tempting to keep your baby in a sleeping bag for as long as possible to stop her trying to stand up at night. But as we've said before, the standing-up-in-the-cot phase is short-lived and it's actually kinder to your baby not to restrict her when she's so excited about her new standing skills.

We'd suggest that you start using blankets or a baby quilt at night, and if your baby is particularly active and continually kicks it off, you could put a fleece sleep suit (available from baby shops and large supermarkets) over the top of her cotton one on cold nights. As with a baby sleeping bag, you'll be zipping her into something cosy, so hopefully she'll find this settling.

FEEDING

Now that your baby is 1 she can have some foods that she wasn't previously allowed, such as honey (this can cause botulism in the under-1s) and soft-boiled, fried and poached eggs (under-1s are only allowed hard-boiled eggs or scrambled because of the food-poisoning risk).

The big change this month is that if you're bottle-feeding then you can finally give cow's milk to your baby instead of messing about mixing up formula. She should, however, switch to a cup instead of drinking from a bottle to minimize the risk of tooth decay (more on this in Month 16).

Do note that babies need full-fat cow's milk (rather than skimmed or semi-skimmed) because it contains more vitamin A and D than skimmed, and also the extra fat is necessary for brain development. The exception to this is overweight babies, who should be given semi-skimmed milk, but seek advice from your health visitor before you switch.

Unlike formula milk, cow's milk doesn't contain iron, which is why it's not recommended as a drink for babies younger than 12 months. It's also important to limit your baby to around 400ml a day (a little less than a pint), including what she has on her cereal. This will give her two to three feeds a day. Drinking around 400ml of cow's milk will give your baby her recommended daily allowance of calcium but won't fill her up so much that she's not interested in eating other nutritious foods, especially those rich in iron.

Some experts recommend continuing with formula after the age of 1 to ensure that your baby gets enough iron. Unless your baby has a medical condition and has been recommended by her doctor to continue with formula, we don't think this is necessary and it could actually mask any eating problems which would otherwise need addressing.

Still Breastfeeding?

Do continue, because your baby will benefit – one breastfeed equates to roughly one portion of calcium-rich food. But you could also give her a cup of cow's milk each day, as it's also full of bone-building calcium and it's a good idea to let her get a taste for it. Don't let your baby have more than three milk feeds a day in total (breastmilk and cow's milk) – again, it's important that she doesn't fill up on milk at the expense of other foods.

Getting Enough Calcium

If your baby isn't keen on the taste of milk, she can have milk on her breakfast cereal and also get her calcium from yoghurt, mild cheese, custard, rice pudding, pulses such as chickpeas and lentils, dried apricots, sesame seeds (for example, tahini paste) or tinned fish with soft bones such as sardines. Aim at between three and four small portions a day of calcium-rich food (including milk).

Vitamin Drops

We mentioned vitamin drops in Month 8, and if you're not giving them to your baby yet then it's time to start. The Department of Health recommends that all children aged 1 to 5 are given vitamins A, C and D. This ensures that even fussy toddler eaters get their nutrients.

Do note that the vitamin drops taste horrid, so you may need to sneakily add them to your baby's food.

As we've mentioned before, you can buy NHS Healthy Start children's vitamin drops from chemists (£1.77), or you can get them free if you are on

Income Support. Speak to your health visitor or visit www.healthystart.nhs.uk.

- Vitamin A boosts immunity and is good for the skin and vision. It can be found in liver, milk, eggs, oily fish (for example mackerel and salmon), milk, cheese and yoghurt.
- Vitamin C helps iron absorption and wound healing. Good sources include oranges, blueberries, red peppers, strawberries and kiwi fruit.
- Vitamin D is needed for healthy bones and teeth and is found in only a few foods including milk, eggs and oily fish (for example mackerel and salmon). Most of our vitamin D is made in our skin when it's exposed to sunlight. But in the UK winter sun isn't always adequate, especially if your baby is dark-skinned.

DEVELOPMENT AND PLAY

Talking

Your baby's understanding gets even better this month and she will start to be able to follow simple instructions. Try asking her to 'say Bye-bye' and she may wave and perhaps even say 'Bye.' You can also ask her to 'clap hands,' 'push the train,' 'pick up teddy' and so on.

Some babies will have a couple of words by their first birthday, and if your baby has started to talk, she'll quickly build her vocabulary.

If your baby hasn't said anything yet it's worth getting her hearing checked if you haven't done so already. If it is OK, then you have absolutely nothing to worry about because she's completely within the developmental norm (doctors won't worry until a child is 18 months old and still hasn't said anything).

As we've mentioned before, reading stories together, responding to her babble and any attempts at words, singing with her and pointing things out when you're walking can all help your child learn to talk.

MILESTONES

(All babies are different – you probably won't be able to tick everything on this list.)

☐ *Passing* – if you ask your baby to give you something she has in her hand, she may pass it to you because she's now able to make a conscious decision to let go of objects.

☐ *Scribbling* – some babies will be able to hold a crayon and make a few faint marks on some paper, or perhaps hold a paint brush and smear a few colours. Most babies are only interested for a couple of minutes at this age, and some won't be interested at all just yet. But from now on, watch out for your baby getting hold of your pens and marking walls, carpets and books – keep pens out of reach.

☐ *Fantasy play* – your baby may start to feed her teddies and give them drinks from about this age. She may also hold your mobile phone to her ear, or pretend to eat toy food. As your baby starts imaginary play she will also learn to use language to play – this happens any time between now and about 18 months.

☐ *More dexterous* – her movements are now more refined and effortless than when she first started picking things up as she develops more control.

☐ *Grabbing without looking* – instead of the laborious eye-hand coordination your baby managed at 6 months, she can now reach for something while looking the other way.

☐ *Can hold three bricks* – if your baby is holding a brick or toy in each hand, you can pass her a third object and she'll put one of her toys on the crook of the opposite arm, then take the new object with her free hand.

☐ *Can track moving objects well* – your baby started to be able to track moving objects with her eyes at about 6 months, but is even better at this now she is mobile and able to turn to watch things. You can encourage this by pointing out things like fire engines and birds. Do note that if your baby doesn't seem to be tracking moving objects by now, you need to get her checked out.

☐ *Permanent eye colour* – by now your baby will have her permanent eye colour. In the early months a baby's eye colour can change, perhaps from blue to brown. But there is unlikely to be any further change now that your baby is 1.

WHEN TO WORRY

Babies should be moving by now – either crawling, creeping, bottom-shuffling or even rolling. It doesn't matter how, but your baby should be able to get herself around the room. If she's still not mobile, it's worth getting her checked out by your health visitor or doctor.

Babies should be completely ambidextrous until they are about 18 months. If you notice that your baby is very much left- or right-handed, it can indicate problems at this age.

Also, if your baby can't yet pick up tiny objects with the tip of her thumb and index finger it can sometimes indicate problems with her fine motor skill development.

SAFETY TIP OF THE MONTH

Ensure that new birthday toys carry a CE mark (Conformité Européene). This certifies that a product has met the health, safety and environmental requirements of the European Union. Also check the age – toys suitable for 3+ usually include small parts which your baby may want to put in her mouth. Also check that ride-on toys don't topple over if your baby uses them to pull herself up to standing.

WHEN TO SEE THE DOCTOR ✚

Viral-induced wheezing

This begins with a cold and cough which is followed by wheezing – a whistling sound when your baby breathes out that can go on for a couple of months. A viral-induced wheeze is very common and is caused by the narrowing of the airways due to mucus or inflammation after an infection. This is particularly common in the under-2s, especially in boys. Some 25 per cent of children under the age of 5 will be affected, but most will grow out of it as their respiratory system matures.

If your baby develops a wheeze, then see your doctor; he or she may prescribe Ventolin and/or Atrovent which treat asthma and breathing problems. Your baby is too young to use an inhaler, so you can give her these drugs using something called a 'spacer' device – a large plastic container that fits around your baby's nose and mouth – and you pump the inhaler into the device at the other end.

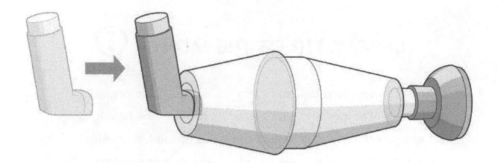

Spacer device – this fits over your baby's face so she can inhale medicine.

If you're still breastfeeding then keep going, because this will help protect your baby against allergy-induced asthma later on. And do avoid exposing your baby to smoky atmospheres – if you're a smoker, try to give up.

Please note: When we refer to 'asthma' we're talking about wheezing that is triggered by an allergy. This doesn't affect babies until they are about 2, and we cover it in Month 22.

WHAT'S HAPPENING TO MUM AND DAD

If you're back to work, your partner will be even more involved with looking after your baby – perhaps having sole charge for a day or an evening a week.

It's important to realize that there's more than one way to look after a baby. You can leave lists and timetables and this will probably help your partner, but at the end of the day he's not you and will do things differently – you should allow him this freedom.

Dads are more inclined to spend time playing than tidying, and water games at bathtime will probably be very lively, which is great for building water confidence.

Where dads really come into their own is mealtimes. Dads aren't usually bothered if their baby doesn't want to eat all her dinner and will reason, quite rightly, that 'she isn't hungry'. Mums, on the other hand, can sometimes be overanxious when it comes to feeding and have an almost primeval instinct to urge their baby to eat more. But this can be stressful for your baby, who ideally should be left to decide for herself how much she wants to eat. Men tend to find this easier than women, who often worry, unnecessarily, that their baby hasn't eaten 'enough'. (More on this next month.)

PLANNING AHEAD

When it comes to first shoes, it's actually better to be disorganized than to plan ahead. So don't rush to the shoe shop as soon as your baby starts walking. Ideally you shouldn't put your baby in shoes until she can walk well – a good 6 weeks after her first steps (see Month 14). This is because the bones in babies' feet are very soft and need time to develop, so your baby is better off perfecting her walking skills barefoot than in shoes, as this allows her to spread her toes for balance and also strengthen her arches.

In the meantime, if your baby's feet are cold, we suggest socks – just make sure they aren't too tight. Socks are also OK for taking a few early steps outdoors, say in the park in the summer – but remember to pack spares in case your baby loses one or they get wet.

Some mums prefer the extra warmth of baby shoes which are a bit like slippers – your baby won't need to be measured for these; you buy them by 'age' from baby shops. Baby shoes can work well in winter as long as they are soft and not rigid. But there's no need to bother with pre-walking or cruising shoes (a soft version of 'real' shoes). Even reputable shoe shops will try to sell you these – they cost about £30 and are more rigid than baby shoes, but they won't help your baby to walk – your baby is better off barefoot.

MONTH 13

INTRODUCTION

This month your baby is due for her MMR vaccine to protect her against measles, mumps and rubella. It's important to get your baby vaccinated quickly because the immunity acquired from Mum starts to wear off around now and your baby will be unprotected. There's no point having this vaccine earlier, however, because babies still have antibodies from their mother.

Your baby will also be given a pneumococcal booster vaccine to protect against pneumonia, septicaemia and meningitis – she would have had this already at 2 and 4 months. The big challenge at this vaccination session is that there are two injections and your baby is old enough to realize what's going on. Most babies of this age cope reasonably well with the first injection, but become pretty upset and scared when they realize it's going to happen again.

There's no way around this – your baby will almost certainly cry. But as we suggested last month, you can prepare your baby by telling her what's going to happen, and again you can produce a new toy as a distraction. But most important, let the nurse or doctor do the job as quickly as possible, and then give your baby lots of comfort afterwards.

Some parents hesitate about having the MMR done at all because of the stories about the link with autism. If you're concerned, have a look at http://news.bbc.co.uk/2/hi/health/1808956.stm, which shows the history of research into MMR and its safety, and is very reassuring. And just for the record we, the authors of this book, have had all six of our children vaccinated against MMR as a single vaccine, and indeed have had our children receive all the recommended immunizations for babies and children. We don't recommend separate measles, mumps and rubella vaccines because, unlike MMR, these vaccines aren't licensed and aren't made in this country so we have no handle on their standard.

SLEEP

Aim: uninterrupted night sleep 11–12 hours
To bed early – about 7 or 8 p.m.
One or two naps: *sometimes a short (20- to 30-minute) morning nap, plus a longer lunchtime nap (2–3 hours)*
A total of 14 hours' sleep

Most babies of this age have a total of around 14 hours' sleep including daytime naps. Over the next few months you will notice that your baby starts to need slightly less sleep during the day, dropping her morning nap (if she hasn't done so already), and sleeps for a little longer at night.

So at the moment she may have, say, 11 hours of sleep at night and a total of 3 hours of naps, but this will soon switch to 12 hours at night and a 2-hour lunchtime nap during the day.

Your baby's lunchtime nap will become more important once it becomes her only daytime sleep, and she'll probably go down for it more easily because she's more tired. Putting your baby down at about the same time each day will teach her body that it's sleep time and she'll start to feel tired in anticipation.

Lots of parents relish this 2-hour break in the middle of the day. However, the downside can be that you have to plan your day around it to some extent, because most babies can't go entirely without their daytime nap until they are at least 2 years old.

You probably won't be able to get away with skipping the daytime nap for quite a while yet without risking your child becoming extremely over-tired and fractious.

To give yourself more flexibility you can encourage your baby to nap in her buggy – even if she goes off a bit later than usual, this should be enough to take the edge off her tiredness in the afternoon. And there's no rule that says that your baby has to have her nap after lunch. If you're in the habit of going out with your baby at lunchtime and she seems happy enough to have a good sleep in the morning – that's fine. If she's getting a regular, undisturbed sleep each day, it doesn't matter if her nap is in the morning or the afternoon. In this book we've guided parents towards an afternoon nap simply because it is often easier to get babies and toddlers to go to sleep at this time.

If you're going somewhere by car, your baby may well drop off on the way – if she has about an hour's sleep, this should be enough to get her through the day without her lunchtime nap. She may become lethargic and miserable during the time she's supposed to be sleeping, and then perk up at around the time she usually wakes. But she'll then become tired again at teatime and be quite cranky.

Troubleshooting

My baby has just dropped her morning nap but only sleeps for 45 minutes at lunchtime

There are several things you can try. First, give your baby some milk, either breast- or cow's milk, after her lunch. Also, babies have sleep cycles of around 45 minutes, after which they wake for a few seconds before drifting back again for their next sleep cycle. Sometimes babies don't drift back again very easily and will think it's time to get up. Try helping your baby back to sleep again, perhaps rubbing her tummy, saying 'shhh', or whatever technique you use to get your baby off.

The idea is to get your baby into the habit of having a long lunchtime nap. Once this is established she will be more likely to resettle herself in between sleep cycles because her body will actually feel tired. And of course you can gradually reduce the help you give her getting her back to sleep (as described in Month 7) once she is used to sleeping for longer.

FEEDING

If you haven't been able to face giving your baby her own spoon until now, then it's time to start. Developmentally she's old enough and has the necessary skills – all she needs is the opportunity to practise. She'll have great fun playing with the spoon, dipping it in her food, and sometimes getting it in her mouth. Try not to wipe her mouth until the end of the meal, because this will annoy her – also, rubbing her chin will stimulate dribble.

Your baby will probably insist on feeding herself around now, anyway, and you just have to accept that mealtimes will be particularly slow and messy for the next 3 months, by the end of which she will be pretty good at feeding herself. You'll probably see a small improvement every week.

There's a chance your baby won't want to feed herself, and this may be because she is particularly hungry so finds it frustrating not being able to eat quickly – in which case don't hesitate to help her. Or perhaps you give her more attention when you're feeding her, so try sitting with her and watching and encouraging as she attempts to spoon-feed herself. If she still doesn't want to feed herself, simply try giving her a spoon again in a month or so – she'll change her mind eventually as long as you don't let her think it's a big issue.

And, as if mealtimes weren't challenging enough, your baby will probably make incomprehensible demands about the food, drinks and particular spoons, cups or plates that she wants passed to her. And she's bound to get angry if you get it wrong. Again, this will improve over the next few months as your baby's speech develops.

Do note that babies in large families often learn to feed themselves earlier because they get fed up with waiting for Mum to spoon them their food. So we suggest that you give your baby a spoon and let her get on with it.

Your baby is also ready to drink from a cup with no lid, if she's not done so already. As we've suggested in previous months, put just a centimetre of water in at a time, then it doesn't matter if it spills – at this age she'll probably make a pretty good attempt at drinking from it and will love the fact that it's 'grown up', although she won't be able to put the cup down gently enough to avoid spilling it until she is about 18 months. In the meantime, your baby is quite likely to drop it on the floor unless you're on hand to take it from her, which is why we suggest sticking to just a centimetre of water.

Do note that lots of babies still use beakers with lids at this age, particularly if they are drinking anything other than water. Just ensure that your baby has a free-flow beaker (the sort that leaks if you turn it upside down) rather than a non-spill beaker which only works if your baby sucks it.

Not Eating Enough

Lots of mums worry that their toddler hardly seems to eat anything, but toddlers don't actually need that much to eat. Many of them eat two meals a day well and will just pick at their third meal. This is fine.

One of the reasons parents worry is that they compare what their toddler eats to what they eat themselves, and it can seem very little. But a 10kg toddler needs just 950 calories a day – and if they're drinking the recommended pint of milk (370 calories) this leaves 580 calories a day for food. That's less than a third of what Mum might eat when she's on a diet. (Breastfed babies will probably get around the same number of calories – 370 – from breastmilk each day.)

There's no point trying to count your baby's calories, because so much food gets wasted, spat out and thrown on the floor that it's pretty much impossible. Also there's a danger of becoming obsessed and worrying even more about how much your toddler is – or isn't – eating.

The take-home message is that most babies don't eat much and there's probably no need to worry. Checking your child's weight each month is the only objective way of knowing if she's eating enough.

DEVELOPMENT AND PLAY

Talking

Some babies will have a few words by now, although they probably won't say them particularly clearly yet. Others still won't be able to say anything. But most babies will be better than ever at making themselves understood without resorting to crying. So now your baby will be able to tug at your clothes when she wants attention, point to things she wants, push away things she doesn't and shake her arms and yell with frustration if you don't understand her first time around. She'll make enough fuss to ensure you keep guessing until you get it right.

Babies love repetition, so your baby may want you to read her the same story or sing the same song again and again. Hearing the same story repeatedly is predictable and comforting for her. Also, repetition is part of the learning process, so try and be patient, however tedious it gets.

MILESTONES

(All babies are different – you probably won't be able to tick everything on this list.)

☐ *Puts things into containers* – your baby has been able to use her hands independently since she was about 10 months, and now that she's more

WHEN TO

We suggested a few simple ey

check your baby's eyes again t

following, see your doctor:

- Your baby's eyes don't mo
  sometimes she appears to

- Your baby seems indiffere
  objects.

Also, if your baby still become

such as sirens, vacuum cleaner

with, it can sometimes be a sig

spectrum, so worth getting it

SAFETY TIP O

Doors and fingers

Once your baby is on the mov

they can blow shut in the wind

or toddles through a doorway.

fingers. This is a particularly co

most hurt their finger in a doo

damage, even losing fingers.

dexterous she'll have fun putting small objects into a container. At mealtimes she may put peas into her cup, or you could give her a box to put bricks into.

☐ *Enjoys singing* – if your baby hears a song often enough she'll come to recognize it and will love joining in with the actions (with your help) and perhaps even singing the odd word or two. So try 'row, row the boat', 'wind the bobbin up' and any other songs with actions that you know. You could think about joining a parent-and-toddler singing group – your baby is old enough to enjoy it.

☐ *Dribbles less* – as babies gain control over their tongue they start to dribble less about now. Some babies, however, continue to drool because they simply have a lot of saliva, and will carry on dribbling until they are old enough to be socially aware – this can be as old as 3½.

☐ *Clings to your legs* – this is a phase that begins shortly before babies get walking. Your baby may crawl up to you then use your legs to pull to standing. Over the next few months you will sometimes find getting around the kitchen quite torturous because you've got a baby firmly attached to your leg – even after she can walk, your child will still use your leg for balance and, eventually, just comfort.

☐ *Is absorbed by toys* – your baby was probably given lots of birthday presents last month, and she will have played happily with these for about 15 minutes at a time. We suggest that you rotate her toys, boxing some away and producing 'new' toys each week. At this age your baby's short-term memory is still quite undeveloped so she probably won't remember ever having seen the toys before. It will be like a birthday every week (for you, too, because your baby will be totally absorbed for a while playing with her 'new' toys).

☐ *Takes off socks* – your ba
pulling off loose socks and oth
if you get annoyed, she'll love
having her socks put back on
on her hand and making a joke
foot. You can also use hats wit

☐ *Objects to having her nappy*
increasingly lively and wriggly
still frustrating. This will contir
starts to gradually improve. Ir
your baby's attention so that
to wriggle away. You can mak
particular faces for changing ti
can help, as can giving her a s
not familiar with can work. Y
magazine with a bright pictur
clean nappy or a hair brush. /
parts (see next month) this ca
you can say, for example, 'Wh
touches her nose than grabs a
onto all fours for a nappy char
as if she's lying down, but it's p
get bored after a few weeks. Th
and try to avoid it becoming a

Babies find doors fascinating once they're on the move, and the easiest answer we've found are foam horse shoes that slot over the edge of the door to stop it from shutting completely. Available from Boots for a few pounds, these take two seconds to put on and take off, so you could pop one onto a back door when it happens to be open, and whip it off whenever you want to shut it completely.

WHEN TO SEE THE DOCTOR ✚

Tonsillitis

Because your baby will probably be mixing with lots of other children by now, she's more likely than ever to pick up throat infections.

The key signs of tonsillitis are a sore throat and swollen tonsils. It is usually caused by a viral infection. Tonsils are made of lymphoid tissue, which swells when fighting viruses and bacterial infections.

Tonsillitis will usually clear up by itself within a few days, and you can give your child Calpol and baby ibuprofen in the meantime, along with plenty of fluids and easy to swallow foods such as jelly, yoghurt and ice cream. Children this age are too young for throat lozenges.

Even if there is no infection, tonsils can be quite large at this age because they actually continue to grow until children are 8, then they start to shrink. So do take a look at your child's tonsils when there's no infection so that you know how big they are – you can do this by persuading your child to open her mouth and say 'aaah', which flattens the back of the tongue. If your child doesn't want to cooperate, don't force her.

Sometimes the cause of tonsillitis is streptococcus bacteria, which leads to strep throat. In this case you will need to take your child to the doctor for antibiotics. The big giveaway with bacterial infections is a fever, so if your child's temperature is 38°C or higher, then take her to the doctor. Although strep throat can often get better on its own, there is a risk of it turning into a more severe infection.

These days tonsils are rarely removed unless they became so big that they obstruct the airway. And, very occasionally, tonsils are removed if they are chronically infected.

WHAT'S HAPPENING TO MUM AND DAD

Lots of mums delay making the decision about when and indeed if they are going to go back to work until the last minute. But the 1-year deadline is now over, so you'll have made your decision by now. Perhaps Dad has given up work and you've gone back to work (more on stay-at-home dads next month).

But if you've finally handed in your notice so that you can be a stay-at-home mum, then you and your partner may be feeling a little mixed at the moment. Of course you'll be delighted you're going to be spending so much time with your baby, but there's obviously more financial pressure on Dad and less money now you're down to one income. And Mum may be having pangs about her lost work camaraderie, perhaps missing the office and even dressing up in heels and a suit.

If this is you, then it's best to try to forget about the office and get on and enjoy your baby – the next year is going to be very exciting. It's also worth finding a few other mummy friends to meet with because it's useful to have the support of people with children of a similar age. No doubt you know a few already, but some of them may well have gone back to work recently. You can keep up your network of mums by joining toddler groups, as your baby is now old enough to enjoy these.

If you're back at work, then you've probably discovered that guilt can be a big issue for working mums. Plenty of people will tell you over the years how much children benefit from having a stay-at-home mum. You could argue that you'd rather put a roof over your child's head than play bricks with her, especially if you're a single parent (more on single parents in Month 15). You could also point out that anecdotal evidence suggests that stay-at-home mums yell more at their kids and are less patient than working mums. Even in traditional societies, the extended family gives mothers lots of help and respite.

There are no easy answers to this ongoing dilemma, and no right or wrong way. At the end of the day, we all just muddle through and try to do what is best for ourselves and our own family.

PLANNING AHEAD

Now that your baby has turned 1, you may well be planning your next baby. If this is the case, then chances are you'll get pregnant within the next few months or so, and your first child will be about 2 when your new baby is born – a very popular age gap.

Of course, not all couples manage to conceive easily a second time (more on secondary infertility in Month 19). But whatever you're planning, you'll probably be having a clear-out of old clothes and toys around now – a year's worth takes up a lot of space. If you're planning to have more children then you'll obviously be packing stuff away for future babies. Take a little time to organize and label things into age order – 'newborn clothes', '0–3 months', 'bedding for Moses basket', and so on. This will make things slightly less chaotic when baby number two arrives. Also, if you're heavily pregnant you may well be sending someone else up to the loft to get the baby stuff down, and it will help if it's well labelled.

MONTH 14

INTRODUCTION

Traditionally, chubby babies have been thought of as healthy. Indeed, a bit of spare fat to tide them through illness or famine could be the difference between life and death. But today lots of babies are actually overweight and are storing up serious health problems for later in life.

This is a particularly difficult problem for mums to face up to, and if your health visitor tries to suggest that your beautiful baby is fat, you'll probably feel outraged and somewhat defensive. But before you dismiss her as not knowing what she's talking about, do have a look at your baby's red book and you'll see her progress on the weight chart compared to other babies her age. Perhaps she used to be about average and, since weaning, she's jumped up a couple of centiles, which suggests she's eating too much. By all means get a second opinion, but the likelihood is that your baby is overweight – this is a very common problem these days. And you can forget about your baby being 'big boned' or having 'big parents' – that would account for her being tall, not heavy. If she's off the scale of the weight chart, then she is almost certainly overweight.

The hardest step is accepting that your baby needs to lose weight, but once you've done that the rest is fairly straightforward – easier in many ways than controlling your own weight.

There are plenty of reasons why babies are overweight. Drinking too much milk can be a culprit because babies can get calories more quickly and easily from milk than from solids. Comfort drinking from a night bottle is particularly likely to cause obesity.

Another reason is snacking and grazing – it's easy to calm a crying baby by handing her rice cakes or biscuits in her buggy. We've all done this from time to time, but if it becomes a habit it's a problem. The golden rule is to limit your baby to no more than two snacks a day.

A third reason is giving your baby unhealthy food. Babies naturally stop eating when they're full, and are better than adults at doing this. But they may ignore their satiety signals if given sweet or salty foods like chocolate and crisps. A fourth reason is that your baby is drinking too many sweet drinks such as juice and squash, which can pack in the calories.

So sit down with your health visitor and analyse together the reason why your baby may be eating too many calories. Then re-plan what you give her to eat. Your baby might not need to lose weight at this age, in which case she'll simply be given an eating plan to ensure that she doesn't put it on so quickly, and will soon be a more healthy weight for her age.

In a nutshell, your baby will probably be limited to no more than a pint of formula or cow's milk a day, three healthy meals, and two healthy snacks, plus water to drink.

SLEEP

Aim: uninterrupted night sleep 11–12 hours
To bed early – about 7 or 8 p.m.
One or two naps: sometimes a short (20- to 30-minute) morning nap, plus a longer lunchtime nap (2–3 hours)
A total of 14 hours' sleep

You may notice that your baby sleeps more deeply than she used to and is less sensitive to being woken up. Your baby's sleep pattern is maturing and several things are happening.

First, she's having more deep sleep than she used to – we all have several sleep cycles a night consisting of deep and light sleep, and as babies get older, the proportion of deep sleep increases. The amount of deep sleep that your baby has each night will increase further – this partly explains why broken nights become less of an issue for parents as their children get older.

Your baby's sleep cycles will also be getting longer, which means there will be fewer periods of light sleep when she can potentially be woken by noise or disturbance. Again, this bodes well for her ability to sleep through the night.

It's also worth noting that your baby will sleep more soundly during the first half of the night than the second. This is because the pattern of each of her sleep cycles changes throughout the night. In her first sleep cycle she'll have lots of deep sleep followed by just a few minutes of lighter, dreaming sleep. But by the end of the night the lighter dreaming sleep will last much longer (this is why we dream in the morning before we get up).

Practical Applications

Now that your baby's sleep pattern is maturing, you'll be able to put her to bed in the car and drive late at night if you're going on holiday, or visiting grandparents or friends. Driving at night with small children is a huge advantage – there's no crying or car-sickness when they're asleep.

Having this flexibility will mean that you can stay out with family and friends until your child's bedtime, probably around 7 p.m., rather than having to rush back for her tea and bath.

You don't necessarily need to bath your baby if you're with friends, just change her nappy, wipe her hands and face, put her in her sleep suit and clean her teeth. Putting your baby to sleep in the car means you don't have to go through the bedtime story and settling routine – you'll no doubt relish the 'night off'.

When you get to your destination it will take a little time to settle your baby into her bed. But do persevere, because by the time your baby is 2 it's likely you'll be able to carry her from the car into bed without her significantly waking up. It's also worth noting that, because babies and young children sleep more deeply during the first half of the night than the second, if you time your arrival before midnight it can make a big difference to how easily they settle into bed.

Troubleshooting

When we wake up our baby to put her in the car at night to go to my parents, she doesn't go back to sleep for ages

Some babies get excited by being hoisted out of their beds and plonked in the car in the middle of the night. You'll find that as she gets older she'll get used to this pattern, and also as her sleeping pattern matures she'll find it difficult to stay awake for so long.

If she's distressed, you could try getting her ready for bed then putting her to 'bed' in the car when you're ready to set off, explaining that you're going to Grandma and Grandpa's house. Tuck her up in a blanket and pop in her favourite toy to cuddle and she may find the experience less disorientating than being put to sleep in her cot and then later moved into the car.

FEEDING

Eating three meals a day at around the same times each day will help establish life-long healthy eating habits. Your toddler will be hungry at mealtimes and this means she will probably eat well when she sits down for a meal. The downside is that she'll find it difficult to wait if her meal is late for some reason, even by a few minutes.

As she gets older she'll be able to last a little longer without food and won't start throwing tantrums if she's not fed on the dot. But in the meantime, be patient, because her stomach is very small and she genuinely finds it difficult if she's not fed close to her normal mealtimes. If you're out and you know she's going to be fed a bit late, have a snack handy. Try not to resort to giving your toddler a pre-meal 'snack' too often, though, or you could easily slip into the grazing habit (see below).

Another option if you're cooking and it's taking longer than anticipated is to give your toddler vegetables to munch on – these are healthy, not too filling and are often ready before the rest of the meal. This is also a good way to encourage children to eat vegetables, and you can continue giving your toddler a piece of broccoli or some raw pepper as a 'starter' for years to come (more on vegetables and toddlers in Month 23).

Grazing

A three-meal-a-day habit isn't always established early on, and some toddlers can end up grazing throughout the day. It's certainly an easy way to feed a small child – leaving sandwiches or breadsticks out for her to help herself to, or perhaps giving her a little snack every time she gets a bit cranky, particularly when she's in the buggy. She'll be so full that you won't have to bother with lunch.

We're all for shortcuts and anything that makes life with a small child easier, but the potential problem with all-day grazing is that your baby won't learn to sit down to a meal, and will start to demand to be drip-fed snacks all day long. This can become more of a problem once your baby is walking, because she will be able to walk around clutching bits of food.

There's no doubt that sitting down to a meal has benefits. First, your baby will eat better food – it's not easy grazing on things like fish, meat and vegetables, but very easy to give her biscuits, chocolate buttons and chips on the run. Also, at mealtimes she'll be focusing on her food, so is more likely to stop eating when she's full. And then there's the social aspect of learning to enjoy sitting down to eat with the family.

Breaking the Grazing Habit

Some mums describe their baby as a 'grazer' and are sure that from birth this has been her eating pattern (lots of little milk feeds). But we're convinced that all babies can be taught to eat three meals a day with a couple of snacks in between.

Do be prepared for your toddler to get upset and cross as you change her eating pattern, but persevere because, in the long term, she will benefit.

Begin by cutting back her snacks to just two a day – perhaps some fruit or a fromage fraîs mid-morning, and a piece of toast mid-afternoon (see more snack ideas below). Your toddler will become hungry and demand more, so it will help if you're busy and perhaps doing something a bit different to take her mind off her hunger. Then at lunchtime sit her in her highchair and give her a lunch you know she likes. Do the same at dinnertime, and continue this pattern until she stops asking for constant snacks in between meals.

It won't be easy because your baby will get upset and you'll be tempted to give her something to eat to quieten her. But do try to resist. The first three or four days will be the hardest, after which your child will hopefully feel less hungry in between meals as her appetite adjusts to her new eating pattern.

Once your baby is having three highchair meals a day, you'll probably find that she eats reasonably quickly because she's hungry. There will be times when she hardly eats a thing at mealtimes, but resist the temptation to fill her up on snacks later. Give her a snack by all means, but make sure it is something quite small so that she'll be hungry again by her next meal.

Snacks

Snacking is important for toddlers because they have high energy requirements but small stomachs – a couple a snacks a day is reasonable. It's easy to stick to healthy snacks at this age because your child is too young to be demanding crisps and biscuits. So make the most of it before she starts demanding 'treats' and give her healthy foods like little sandwiches made with egg or peanut butter, a small yoghurt, a banana, a satsuma, a peach, some sliced apple, a small handful of raisins or chopped dried apricot, some strawberries or a piece of toast.

DEVELOPMENT AND PLAY

Talking

You can increase your child's vocabulary by offering her choices – 'Do you want a peach or a banana?' Your baby may point to her preference, or she may eventually try saying a new word. But in the meantime she'll learn the new words and understand them.

MILESTONES

(All babies are different – you probably won't be able to tick everything on this list.)

☐ *Walking* – lots of babies start to walk this month. Having got the hang of cruising, your baby will find the courage to let go and walk independently. This is an exciting milestone and, once your baby can walk, she won't stop practising however often she topples over. At first she'll probably totter along in a wobbly line towards someone or something she can grasp on to. But she'll soon learn to turn corners and stop without having to hold anything.

☐ *Climbing* – adventurous babies will start to climb around now, even if they can't yet walk – climbing requires less balance because they are using their arms as well as their legs. Less adventurous babies won't climb until they are about 17 months old. But do take precautions (see Safety Tip of the Month, opposite).

☐ *Learning body parts* – your baby is old enough to start learning to point to her tummy, nose, mouth and so on if you spend a bit of time teaching her. This month it's realistic to expect her to just about be able to master one body part. But if she's not interested, leave it for another month.

☐ *Taking her nappy off and playing with poo* – this can happen from around now when your baby has the manual dexterity to actually get her sleep-suit and nappy off. Thankfully, not all babies go through this phase, but if your baby does we suggest putting her sleep-suit on back to front, though to make this work you'll first have to cut the suit toes off. This phase will probably stop by the time your child is 2.

☐ *Kissing back* – some babies will be able to kiss by now, others will take longer. This is one of the most charming developmental milestones and it requires a certain skill for your baby to be able to pucker up her lips. Give her lots of kisses and she'll soon try and copy.

☐ *Biting and hitting* – although unpleasant, this is actually a normal developmental stage and nothing to worry about. We'll talk more about it next month.

☐ *Standing up in her highchair* – as if mealtimes aren't challenging enough at this age, some toddlers start to stand up precariously in their highchairs. You have a few options here: explain that 'standing up is dangerous so you must sit down,' then sit her down. If this doesn't work you could try using highchair straps. But even these won't work for particularly lively toddlers, so you can say, 'Sit down or get down.' Then simply get your toddler down from her highchair even if she hasn't finished her meal. You can pop her back again if she asks – after all, you're not punishing her, just keeping her safe. She'll probably start to tire of this 'game' after a week or so, especially if you don't react strongly but remain matter-of-fact.

WHEN TO WORRY

If your toddler plays extremely well by herself it can sometimes indicate a hearing problem, especially if she doesn't demand much attention from others or seem bothered by what's going on around her. You'll probably think she's a really good baby, but in fact there may be a problem.

SAFETY TIP OF THE MONTH (i)

Your baby may start to climb from around now; lots of babies climb before they learn to walk. Anything that looks vaguely ladder-like, such as towel rails and bookcases, may tempt her to climb up, and she'll soon love climbing up onto tables. You can buy furniture straps (from Mothercare) to secure wobbly furniture (such as a bookcase) to the wall to ensure it doesn't topple over should your little one have a sneaky climb one day. Obviously keep step-ladders out of the way – if they're folded but leaning against a wall it will be very wobbly if your baby manages to have a go at climbing up. As for towel rails, you can hang towels on them to disguise them a little, but the best answer is to get into the habit of keeping the bathroom door shut – especially if the towel rail is heated.

WHEN TO SEE THE DOCTOR ✚

Facial bruising

Once your baby is on the move she's bound to have a few bumps, particularly when she starts to stand. Occasionally she'll bruise her face, usually because she topples over and bashes against something hard, like furniture. Do cover sharp corners, and remove any wobbly furniture that might fall over easily. Also, encourage your baby to practise her walking on carpet rather than a hard floor, which might be slippery, and get into the habit of closing drawers, cupboards, the dishwasher and anything else that she might run into or that might trip her up. As well as finding it difficult to balance, babies are long-sighted, which means they won't see close objects under their feet very clearly – another reason they fall over a lot.

It's worth noting that facial bruising can be an important indicator of child abuse, particularly before a child is mobile. But before you jump to any conclusions and sack the childminder, do be aware that, although facial bruising is rare in crawlers, it is more common among babies who are cruising and starting to walk.

You can treat bruises by applying ice – a bag of frozen peas wrapped in a tea towel works well. Never apply ice directly to the skin because it may stick and hurt. Another option used by lots of mums is arnica gel, a homoeopathic remedy.

Bruises usually disappear after about a week, and they will be sensitive for a few days, so take care, particularly when pulling vests or jumpers on and off.

Always explain facial bruising to your health visitor, doctor or your baby's nursery carer – otherwise they may start asking questions and perhaps suspect abuse. And if your baby gets several facial bruises while in the care of someone else, it's worth asking how it's happening. Check that the story makes sense and concurs with the injury.

WHAT'S HAPPENING TO MUM AND DAD

If you've taken the decision that Dad stays at home and Mum goes to work, you're certainly not alone. This is becoming a more popular choice and often makes financial sense, as lots of women earn more than their partners these days.

Whatever your reasons for opting for this arrangement, you'll probably run into problems because, as with any arrangement, there will be pros and cons. Here are some suggestions for tackling the most common problems.

Problems Faced by Dad

You may feel isolated and lonely being at home with a toddler day after day. Lots of stay-at-home mums also experience this, and the solution is to build up a network of other parent friends in your area. This is, sadly, easier for women than men because, as a man, you'll still be in the minority at playgroups and toddler activities.

You could sign up for a particular activity such as swimming where the focus will be on following the instructor's directions rather than the social side of things. Or try tracking down other stay-at-home dads in your area – but allow time; it can take a couple of years to build up a really good network of friends.

Problems Faced by Mum

You'll be getting home tired from work and hoping for a tidy home and even dinner on the table. So if your partner isn't unusually domesticated there may well be tension over this. There are several things you can do. First, talk to your partner – you may be able to work something out between you. Perhaps you could take over the bedtime routine and your partner could start on the tidying and cooking.

You should also think back to when you lived alone and would have got home from work and done your own cooking and cleaning – these memories will hopefully make you more tolerant of your current situation. And think about shortcuts – internet food shopping, ready meals, a cleaner.

The other problem you may find is that you feel your child has a stronger bond with her dad than with you. At this age your little one will simply be used to her dad doing everything for her, so will look to him rather than you when she wants something. Hang on to the fact that this will change as soon as your child is no longer dependent on others for every physical need.

PLANNING AHEAD

We mentioned in Month 12 that when your child first learns to walk you can get by with baby shoes, but once she's been walking for 6 weeks, it's time to buy her first pair of 'proper' shoes. These will be the ones you put in your memory box and keep for years.

Children's shoes are expensive, at about £30 a pair. But it's important to get your baby's feet measured at a reputable shoe shop, because badly-fitting shoes could affect how her feet grow and develop. Second-hand or hand-me-down shoes are, unfortunately, out of the question. You could, however, try the outlet shops of good chains, where the same shoes are a little cheaper, or buy during the store sales – though, frustratingly, she may not need new shoes at this time.

Don't buy sandals for your child because the skin on her bare feet is very soft and will be irritated by the sandals. It's better to keep children in cotton socks and shoes, however hot the weather. The only extra pair of shoes she may need is Wellington boots, which are very cheap. Also it's fine for your child to wear second-hand wellies, as they aren't fitted specifically and your child won't walk far in them, she'll just have fun splashing through puddles.

If your baby happens to go for a paddle in her 'proper' shoes, which is highly likely, stuff them with newspaper so that they don't shrink, then leave them in an airing cupboard or on a radiator overnight.

You'll need to get your baby's feet measured at least every 3 months, although she probably won't need new shoes every time. And don't forget to check her socks – it's important these don't become tight or they'll restrict her foot, and if they're too big they will bunch up and squash her foot.

MONTH 15

INTRODUCTION

Facially, your baby won't change very much from this month onwards. So, apart from her hair, which may still be very fine and short, this is pretty much what your little one is going to look like. If you look back at photos of yourself and your partner you may well see a resemblance in pictures taken at 15 months or older. There's no scientific reason for this, it's purely observational and something that plenty of mothers have noticed. One possible reason is that children start to lose baby fat from the age of around 1.

You will almost certainly be saying 'No' to your toddler by now – when she tries to grab at your hot cup of tea, or if she wants to throw her clothes in the bath. Meanwhile, she's probably highly entertained by your strict voice and stern face, and not taking much notice.

But it's not yet a battle of wills, because your toddler won't have the emotional maturity to defy you until she is at least 2. At the moment she's just experimenting with cause and effect. Also, her brain is still very immature and it will be a few more months before she becomes less impulsive – then she may start to show the very early signs that she is able to listen and think before acting.

So there's no point being too strict or stern at this age; plenty of time for that later. For now you can, very gradually, introduce discipline – perhaps giving a firm 'No' if she's doing something dangerous like reaching towards a hot cup of tea, or if she's hurting another child (more on this next month).

So if your toddler grabs at your tea, move it away and say, 'No, don't touch, it's hot and could hurt you.' By saying 'No' and then following it with an explanation, it will teach your toddler to recognize your tone of voice when you're being firm, and she will understand the gist of your explanation. Try to be consistent and avoid just moving the drink away without saying anything.

We know from experience that there will be days when you seem to be saying 'No' continually and your toddler won't take any notice. Our big tip is don't overuse the word 'No' because it will lose its impact.

So if your baby wants to empty her clothes out of a drawer there's no need to say 'No,' as she's not doing anything dangerous or even wrong – she's simply being curious and having fun. We suggest that if it's going to take you less than a minute to clear up, then let her carry on. But there will be times when you'll be feeling tired and irritable, or you've just tidied her drawer, and there's no way you want her to make another mess. In this case use distraction, such as 'Let's go and have a story.'

And if she's trying to throw her clothes in the bath you can say, 'We don't put our clothes in the bath, we put them in the laundry basket' – then show her what to do. Likewise, 'We don't draw on the wall, we draw on paper' (then give her some paper). Hopefully she'll cooperate because you're effectively showing her what she *should* be doing rather than telling her what she *shouldn't*. You can keep your voice soft and calm, because you're not disciplining your child but teaching her about the world.

Sometimes you'll find yourself in a situation where it's quite difficult to say 'No' to your toddler – for example if she wants a second biscuit at playgroup and the other children are getting one. She'll be genuinely distraught if she sees other children getting biscuits when she's not allowed, and we don't think it's worth the battle. What's likely to happen is that you say 'No, ' then give in when your toddler gets upset – all parents do this from time to time, but you won't do it so often if you don't say 'No' so regularly.

It's definitely better to minimize your 'Nos'. Then in an emergency if your toddler is about to put her hand on a heater and you can't get to her in time, you will yell 'No, that will hurt.' This is more likely to stop her instantly if you've been using your 'Nos' very sparingly.

SLEEP

Aim: uninterrupted night sleep 11–12 hours
To bed early – about 7 or 8 p.m.
One or two naps: *sometimes a short (20- to 30-minute) morning nap, plus a longer lunchtime nap (2–3 hours)*
A total of 14 hours' sleep

Separation anxiety can peak around now and, as we've said before in Month 10, it can affect your baby's sleeping habits.

First, your baby may start to hate it when you leave her room at night. If this happens, then once you've kissed her goodnight, instead of leaving her room you could try staying for a few minutes while you do a bit of tidying. Don't speak to her, just go about your own business. Perhaps you could pop out of the room for a minute or two, and then return to continue tidying. She'll gradually learn that you're nearby, and will feel comforted. The key is not to start giving her extra help to get to sleep such as picking her up and rocking her, or even just stroking her tummy. And don't just sit in her room waiting for her to sleep or she'll soon expect this every night – if you're going in and out of her room, she'll gradually accept you leaving her on her own.

Separation anxiety may also mean that your baby wants you with her if she wakes in the night. A comforter can work well here. If your baby hasn't already got one, do offer her a couple of soft toys at bedtime and she may start to become attached to a particular one. Encourage this bond because your baby can keep her comfort object with her all night and hopefully not need comfort from you. Likewise this can help get her off to sleep at night.

Troubleshooting

Should my baby use a security blanket or toy during the day?
There are both advantages and disadvantages of using a comfort toy or blanket during the day; it really depends on how much your child needs it. The upside is that it will help her to feel safe during the day; this is particularly useful if you're not around, perhaps while she's at nursery or with a childminder.

The obvious downside is that she may lose it, which would cause a lot of distress. To avoid this, you could try to get hold of an identical comforter before the first is lost so that you have a replacement. But if you do this you should alternate the two regularly so that they smell the same and look the same: worn and tatty.

The other disadvantage of using a comforter during the day is that if she's always cuddling a toy it will start to inhibit her play as she gets older, and mixing with other children could be difficult if she's always worrying where her comforter is.

Children get particularly attached to their comforters between the ages of 1 and 3, though most toddlers naturally give them up during the day even if they still cling to them at night. So while it's worth trying gently to persuade your child to leave her comforter in the cot during the day, there's no point insisting if she's adamant. Just keep tabs on it, and remember to tell anyone else who's looking after your baby how important it is.

FEEDING

It's common at this age for children to focus on one food at a time. So if you present your toddler with fish fingers, mash and peas, she may eat all of the peas and want more, but hardly touch the other foods.

She may also go through periods when she eats seemingly excessive amounts of a particular food such as eggs, cheese or perhaps bananas. Or she may veer from protein one week to carbohydrates the next.

You may also notice that your toddler has periods when she seems to eat everything excessively – perhaps she's catching up after being ill, or going through a growth spurt. If your toddler wants more, then let her have as much as she wants. As long as she isn't overweight and she's only demanding healthy foods such as extra portions of Weetabix or boiled eggs, she won't get fat. Grizzling for biscuits while she's bored in her buggy is obviously another matter. It's pretty easy to distinguish between greed and hunger – hunger is demanding second portions of non-sweet foods while sitting in the highchair.

A study in the *New England Journal of Medicine* (1987) found that children instinctively select healthy foods in the absence of adult intervention, and naturally eat the recommended daily amount of nutrients. So unless your child is greedily eating biscuits, or perhaps so much fruit that she's getting diarrhoea, we suggest that you allow her to have her food phases.

You may also find that she's keen to stick to familiar foods at the moment and is reluctant to try anything new. There are two ways around this. First, it's been shown that you need to present a new food at least 15 times to a fussy toddler before she will try it (more on this in Month 23). Secondly, eat it yourself, or better still find other small children to eat it – if your toddler sees cousins or siblings tucking into, say, cucumber, she may well try a bite herself.

DEVELOPMENT AND PLAY

Talking

Most toddlers of this age can say about 10 words, although this is a very rough estimate because language development varies so much between children. And they are unlikely to say these words very clearly. It's still OK if your baby hasn't said a single word yet; rest assured that this doesn't have any bearing on her future development.

Sometimes your toddler won't be able to make herself understood and will get very frustrated as she tries to say a word. For example 'babis' may mean breakfast, 'nok' may mean milk or 'biuit' may mean biscuit – and all of these words may simply mean, 'I'm hungry.' So it's important that you try to learn her language during the early stages of talking, as this will encourage her to talk more. You can say the word back correctly to her, but don't make her repeat it or she'll start to find talking tedious and tiring.

If you can't understand her, simply say, 'I'm sorry, I don't know that word.' This is much better than telling her she's not saying it properly. You could also ask her to point to what she wants and encourage her to communicate in other ways – this won't always work, but it's worth a try.

MILESTONES

(All babies are different – you probably won't be able to tick everything on this list.)

☐ *Builds with big bricks* – we mentioned that at 8 months your baby would be able to release objects randomly, but now she has the fine motor skills to do it with precision and control. This means she is able to put one brick on top of another.

☐ *Investigating* – you will no doubt have heard other mums talk about toddlers being 'into everything'. This peaks around now, and what they're referring to is extreme curiosity coupled with being on the move. So expect your toddler to be pulling books off the shelves, emptying drawers and rooting through cupboards. This can be quite irritating but it is normal for babies of this age to be extremely inquisitive, and all the time she's learning about the world and how things work. Wallets and handbags are very tempting, so keep them out of reach, although you could give her an old purse with a couple of business cards in – but avoid play money (or the real thing) because of the choking hazard. Being able to let go of objects with precision and control makes your baby suddenly a lot more dexterous.

☐ *Crawling again* – lots of babies who have recently learned to walk revert to crawling if they want to move quickly. This is nothing to worry about.

☐ *Overestimates her capabilities* – your baby will be desperate to be independent and do things for herself, but will get very frustrated when she can't. If she's trying to put her shoes on, she'll get annoyed because she can't. And yet if you do it for her she'll also get annoyed. You could try helping her a little bit – showing her how to loosen the fastening and open the shoe so that her foot fits in more easily, then explaining how her toes go in first and she can stand up to push the rest of her foot in. You may have to go through a similar routine if she wants to turn the page of a book, put her coat on or squeeze the shampoo from the bottle. You won't always get it right – nobody does – and it's normal and expected for your little one to become furious with frustration on occasion.

☐ *Tests the boundaries* – babies under the age of 1 think that they're part of their mother, and it's not until the second year that they start to understand they are separate. Part of this process is to test the boundaries. So your baby may happen to throw a toy down the toilet one day, then you'll fish out the toy and tell her not to do it again. So she'll try it again to see if she gets a reaction. She's still too young to be 'naughty', but is testing out cause and effect – how her actions get reactions. There's no point getting cross with a baby at this age because she won't have the reasoning skills to understand why you shouldn't put toys in the toilet. Also her memory is still under-developed, so she will almost certainly forget that she's not supposed to put toys in the toilet, and so does it again.

☐ *Enjoys the company of other children* – your baby may love watching other children, including babies and older children. But she doesn't have the social skills to play with other toddlers yet. She may play alongside others and enjoy their company, but there won't be much interaction.

WHEN TO WORRY

We mentioned waving in Month 10. This is a basic social skill, and if your baby still isn't waving Hello or Goodbye it could indicate that she has social difficulties, or is even on the autistic spectrum. Do see your doctor if you are concerned, especially if your baby isn't nearly as friendly and sociable as others her age.

SAFETY TIP OF THE MONTH ⓘ

Your baby may well like the taste of Calpol and other infant medicine by now, and enjoy the ritual of being given some if she's teething or feeling unwell. But make sure that she doesn't ever help herself and drink some from the bottle. Baby medicine has child-proof caps which are effective, but the problem comes if you don't do them up properly – an easy mistake to make if you've been up in the night giving your baby medicine. You may put the bottle down without thinking and not do the cap up properly – it will click when the child-proof cap is engaged.

This wouldn't have been a problem when your baby was tiny (although not ideal), but now it's dangerous because your baby is on the move, able to stand and reach for things, and extremely curious. The best solution is to take precautions so that your baby never gets to help herself to medicine in the first place, and to keep all medicines in a locked cabinet. But if your child ever does get hold of some medicine, then call NHS direct – 0845 4647, www.nhsdirect.nhs.uk. They will ask how much medicine your baby has had and how much she weighs, then calculate the toxicity levels for her size and assess whether or not she is in any danger.

WHEN TO SEE THE DOCTOR ✚

Breath-holding – reflex anoxic seizure

Breath-holding can occasionally be caused by something called a *reflex anoxic seizure*. This is when small children hold their breath if they get an unexpected fright, shock or pain (the sort of thing that could 'make them jump'). This can also sometimes happen if you raise your voice to tell your baby off. In some children this causes the heart and breathing to stop for several seconds. Your toddler's eyes may roll up into her head and she may go very pale and perhaps blue around the mouth. Her body stiffens and sometimes her limbs jerk. After about 30 seconds, her body relaxes, her heart starts beating again and she will probably regain full consciousness after a couple of minutes (though it can be up to an hour). Your child may feel very emotional and sleepy after an RAS attack, but there is no lasting damage. Such attacks can occur several times a day, week or month.

If your child has such an attack, call for an ambulance then lie your child on the floor on her side checking that she's not choking on dribble or vomit. Talk soothingly – she may be able to hear you. Give her lots of comfort and allow her to sleep afterwards if she wants to – this may be for up to 3 hours.

Sometimes RAS attacks are mistaken for cyanotic attacks, when a child deliberately holds her breath (see below). It's important that you get an accurate diagnosis, and also eliminate epilepsy, which has similar symptoms.

For support and information go to www.stars.org.uk – Syncope Trust And Reflex anoxic Seizures – which also has information on unexplained fainting.

Cyanotic attack

All small children get angry and frustrated sometimes if they can't get their way. Some will express this anger by holding their breath on the out-breath of a long, loud cry. The sudden silence is alarming and guarantees attention, so the child continues to hold her breath for about 20 seconds, and may go blue in the face and even pass out. As soon as she is unconscious she will of course stop holding her breath, breathe again and regain consciousness within about 15 seconds.

This isn't dangerous, but still extremely stressful for parents – do get her checked out by a doctor the first time it happens to put your mind at rest. This will make future breath-holding episodes a lot easier to cope with. The best way to deal with this behaviour is to minimize attention. So if your child is holding her breath, ensure there is nothing sharp or hard for her to fall on, try to catch her as she falls, then lie her flat, checking her airway is clear. When she comes round, don't be cross or sympathetic – try to behave as though you didn't even notice that she passed out. You could also try splashing cold water in her face when she's holding her breath, as this may trigger her to start breathing again. But don't do this once she loses consciousness.

The first time your child has such an attack, do seek medical advice to be sure of the diagnosis. After that you need only see a doctor if she happens to hit her head hard when she passes out.

WHAT'S HAPPENING TO MUM AND DAD

You're into the second year of your baby's life and you and your partner may still be snapping at each other more than you used to before you had a baby. Rather than asking yourself and each other heavy questions about what's happened to your relationship, we suggest you try doing nothing. There's no point analysing your relationship if the underlying problem is exhaustion, and the likelihood is you're both very tired. It's hard looking after a baby, and even if your nights are no longer routinely broken, the fact remains that babies and young children often wake in the night for various reasons.

Relish the days when you've both managed to get a decent amount of sleep – it will be like the old times again and you probably won't be so prickly. And when you go back to being tired and snappy with each other, don't waste time worrying because chances are it's only temporary.

PLANNING AHEAD

Think about rearranging your lower cupboards, drawers and shelves. Your baby will be exploring more than ever from now on and will love emptying things out and rummaging through your things. But if you swap your breakables and anything potentially dangerous (balls of string, scissors, matches) with things like plastic beakers and plates, tea towels and tins, your life will be a lot less stressful because you won't be locking cupboards and saying 'No' so often. Some mums find it works well having one cupboard in the kitchen that their baby is allowed to rummage through – this is an easy way to distract her when she goes for the 'wrong' cupboard.

MONTH 16

INTRODUCTION

You've no doubt introduced your toddler to other children by now, perhaps taking her to playgroups, or she may spend time at nursery or with a childminder during the week. Until now your toddler has probably had a lovely time. But from around this month, lots of small children start to hit, shove, push or even bite (more on biting next month).

It can be quite a shock when your tiny, sweet-looking toddler shows unreserved aggression towards another child. But this is a natural developmental stage – humans are primates, and primates by nature are aggressive and competitive. So you could say that fighting for a particular toy is innate behaviour.

Of course it's up to parents to teach their children to control their violence, and the best way of doing this is to ensure that your child's aggression is never rewarded. So don't let her have the toy she tried to get by hitting, and don't give her too much attention – small children don't discriminate between positive and negative attention from Mum and Dad. Calmly and firmly say something like 'No. We don't hurt, we take turns.' Then you could take her by the hand and show her some other toys. This may not seem much of a 'punishment', but it is an age-appropriate response and gives her a clear and simple message that hitting is wrong.

Do note that developmentally it's inappropriate for a child to be able to share before the age of 2½ – until then she has no sense of anyone else in the world, only a sense of 'self'. Adult supervision is needed to help young children take turns. And in the meantime you can expect a fair bit of hitting and shoving. Console yourself with the fact that nearly all small children fight – some seem to be naturally more violent than others, and most parents know that boys are usually more aggressive than girls. But other than watching closely and intervening quickly, there's not much you can do – just remember that they all do it and they all grow out of it.

It's also comforting to understand *why* toddlers are aggressive – it's basically down to the brain still being very immature. At this age, the primitive rage system in the brain is easily activated and the higher brain isn't yet developed enough to override these feelings. As the brain matures, children have more control over their emotions – you may start to see early signs of control from around 20 months.

Also, as language improves, children are able to explain verbally what they want instead of being physical. In the meantime you could try giving your toddler a calming massage after her bath – use baby lotion or olive oil, warmed in your hands first, and gently massage her legs, arms and tummy, then turn her over to massage her back. Use just enough pressure to indent the skin for the maximum calming effect. Keep your toddler wrapped in a towel and only unwrap the bits you are massaging so that she doesn't get cold. She will probably become restless after a few minutes, in which case, stop – or you'll defeat the purpose of soothing her. And not all children like massage; if this is the case for your baby, then don't do it.

Another relaxing activity is mother-and-toddler yoga – kids love this and you'll feel wonderfully serene afterwards. Half the battle with keeping small children calm is to keep *yourself* calm – which we all know is easier said than done!

You may find there's an expectation from other parents that small children say 'sorry'. Again, this is inappropriate before the age of at least

2, and probably later. It will no doubt make your life easier, however, if you gently put your child through the motions. And of course, you apologizing to the 'victim's' parents will help.

The other playgroup issue you may come across around now is that your child suddenly becomes very clingy. We've mentioned stranger phobia before (Month 10), and the fact that it peaks between 12 and 18 months. So if your child wants to sit on your knee while other children seem to be off on their own having fun, you have absolutely nothing to worry about. Let her stay with you and perhaps go together to find some toys to play with. There's no point pushing her to play on her own, because this clinginess is a normal part of emotional and social development and something that children grow out of.

SLEEP

Aim: uninterrupted night sleep 11–12 hours
To bed early – about 7 or 8 p.m.
One or two naps: sometimes a short (20- to 30-minute) morning nap, plus a longer lunchtime nap (2–3 hours)
A total of 14 hours' sleep

We mentioned in Month 12 that when babies turn 1 they should stop drinking from a bottle and use a cup instead. But lots of babies continue to have a night-time bottle long after this, often well into their third year or older.

This can be a very soothing part of your baby's bedtime routine, and although some people will disapprove of this habit, there's no need to force your toddler to give up her bottle as long as it's not damaging her teeth or being used as a prop to get to sleep.

The big problem with bottle-feeding is that the milk can pool around the teeth, especially if your baby uses her bottle to go to sleep, or worse, sucks on her bottle throughout the night. As well as decay, long-term use can also cause teeth to stick out. The only thing a baby should have during the night is water from a cup – water from a bottle may encourage your baby to wake for the comfort of the bottle rather than because she's thirsty.

It's very common to keep giving your baby milk during the night long after she needs it because it's such an effective way to calm her. But it's important to break this habit because your baby needs to be able to sleep without relying on milk (as we've mentioned in previous months). Also, having milk during the night is bound to affect her daytime appetite, and night bottles are a major cause of obesity.

When a Bedtime Bottle of Milk is OK

Ideally, your baby will have her bottle at around story time then you can clean her teeth afterwards – this cuts the risk of decay.

The next best option is that she drinks her bottle in her cot just before she falls asleep. You'll probably clean her teeth before her bottle rather than afterwards (better than not cleaning them at all), and at least your child won't be sucking on her bottle for hours.

Most children grow out of their bedtime bottles at around 3 when they get frustrated at only being able to drink small amounts of milk at a time – she'll find drinking from a cup much faster and more satisfying.

If you need to change your toddler's milk habits, then take small but firm steps. For example, you could try giving her half her bottle during story time and the other half in her cot, then alter the ratio of amounts until she's having all her milk during story time.

Troubleshooting

Since my baby was ill recently, she won't settle at bedtime
When babies get ill they want a lot of attention – cuddling and rocking to sleep and even bed-sharing. But when they're better they don't willingly

return to old habits. So you have to put in a bit of time re-teaching your baby to get herself to sleep. This is probably the last thing you feel like doing because you would have had lots of bad nights' sleep while your baby was ill. But there isn't an easy answer. The only upside is that it will be much easier to re-teach your baby good sleeping habits than it was first time around. You can use whatever method worked in the past and you'll find that your baby learns a lot more quickly.

FEEDING

Up until now it's probably been fairly easy to feed your child healthy food. She may not always eat what she's given, but she's been too young to demand 'treats' or 'pudding'. You may well have eaten a sneaky chocolate bar or two without her even noticing.

Well, things are about to change. Your child is getting older, and is cleverer and more observant. Any time now she will start to notice if other people are eating something 'better' than she's eating. So if you eat a chocolate biscuit and you give your baby a rice cake, she may complain. Likewise, if you buy an older child an ice cream and give your baby an empty cone, she'll probably object. She may well spit out her pasta and ask for crisps if that's what everyone else is eating.

It's easy to turn this around to your advantage, because now that your baby is keen to copy, if she sees people tucking into healthy food she'll be curious to try some.

It's worth noting that, although your baby understands how delicious 'treats' are, she isn't yet capable of waiting for a treat, so there's no point saying 'Finish your lunch then you can have a yoghurt.' Once she starts thinking about yoghurt, that's all she will want. So don't mention dessert, and certainly don't let her see it. You'll have to wait until she is about 2½ before you can play the 'Eat your broccoli then you can have ice cream' card.

DEVELOPMENT AND PLAY

Talking

In the early stages of learning to talk, your toddler may use the same word to mean different things. For example, 'weeee' can mean pick me up, put me down, I want to get out of my buggy, I want to get in the highchair and so on.

Or if you've got a pet dog, then the word 'dog' may mean any animal. And 'Mummy' can sometimes mean any close family member, so Mummy, Daddy, Grandma, Granddad, the cat and the dog may all be called 'Mummy'.

This is a natural part of language development and your child's vocabulary will soon grow – in the meantime, just enjoy this charming stage because it is very fleeting.

MILESTONES

(All babies are different – you probably won't be able to tick everything on this list.)

☐ *Pointing* – your toddler will point out aeroplanes, dogs, fire engines and anything else that she finds interesting. She may also point out things she wants, such as a drink or a toy.

☐ *Imaginative play* – your child will become particularly interested in playing with 'little people' from around now, as her imagination develops. Perhaps she'll enjoy putting people into toy buses and cars, or giving teddy bears cups of tea. She'll also be enchanted by puppets, and a simple glove puppet will seem real to her.

☐ *Recognizes people from a distance* – your toddler will now get excited if she sees Grandpa or a friend on the other side of the road. As her understanding of the world improves she'll find it easier to recognize people out of context.

☐ *Fascinated with eyes* – toddlers around this age find eyes fascinating and will want to touch yours, as well as poking at the eyes of their toys or pets.

☐ *Wandering off* – most toddlers love the sudden independence of being able to walk competently and will experiment by toddling away from Mum and Dad. Your child's sense of danger starts to develop at about 18 months, but until then, and probably until she's at least 2, be prepared to keep a very close watch, because if she's able to walk then she's likely to wander off.

☐ *'Magnetically' drawn to water* – young children are fascinated by water and from the time they can walk will automatically gravitate to all puddles, taps and sprinklers. Although it can be irritating to see a pair of new leather toddler shoes submerged in a puddle, this is a short-lived phase, so our advice is to get some wellies and try to be charmed by it. Also be aware that your child will happily walk into the sea fully clothed on a winter's day and not stop walking as the sea gets deeper. And likewise she won't be afraid of ponds or swimming pools. Never leave a toddler unattended or unwatched near water.

☐ *Playing with genitals* – lots of children start playing with their genitals around now, usually when they're on the changing table or in the bath. This is nothing to worry about – just as your child may play with her hair or belly button, she'll be interested in her genitals as she becomes more dexterous and also is able to sit up in the bath confidently. There's nothing sexual about this behaviour, it's driven only by curiosity.

WHEN TO WORRY

It's worth seeking medical help if your baby can't stack two cubes yet, as this may indicate late development of her motor skills.

SAFETY TIP OF THE MONTH ⓘ

We mentioned poisoning with overdoses of Calpol and other infant medicines last month. But there are plenty of other substances that can poison and sometimes kill toddlers. It's all very well being vigilant with things like bleach and weed-killer, but the most likely things to poison children are the things that you won't even consider to be particularly dangerous and so may leave lying around. Here's a list of things to watch:

- Iron tablets – known to kill small children if too many are eaten.
- Paracetamol – common but potentially deadly household medicine – just three tablets is enough to kill a 1-year-old.
- Vapour rubs – contain menthol and camphor, which are dangerous if ingested.
- Dishwasher tablets and firelighters – wrapped up like sweets, these are tempting but highly toxic.
- Cigarettes – tobacco is very toxic if eaten.
- Alcohol – glugging neat spirits could be fatal to your toddler, and spirit bottles don't have child-proof caps.
- Tricyclic anti-depressants – very toxic and potentially fatal to small children. Even if you are careful, do be aware that visitors

may have medicines in their coat pockets – easily discovered by a curious toddler.

- Caffeine – it's dangerous for children to 'eat' coffee, so watch out for coffee 'pods' and beans.
- Washing detergent capsules – if children play with these they can pop open and cause chemical eye injuries.

WHEN TO SEE THE DOCTOR ✚

Bow legs, in-toeing and flat feet

Babies' legs are a different shape to a child's and the soft bones naturally straighten and lose any twists as your toddler starts to walk. Most toddlers have straight legs by the time they are 2. In the meantime any irregularities become particularly apparent once your toddler starts to walk; you may notice the following:

Bow legs

Her knees don't touch even when her ankles are together – this is normal before the age of about 2 and will almost certainly correct itself. It's particularly common in babies who walk before 12 months of age, and in babies of African descent. If you notice that one leg seems more bowed than the other or that your child waddles, see your doctor because your toddler may need a splint at night, or special boots. You should also see the doctor if there's a gap of more than 5cm between her knees (measured when lying down).

Bow legs can sometimes be a result of vitamin D deficiency (rickets). So if your baby hasn't had extra vitamins or has been on a restricted diet, see your GP who may arrange a blood test or X-ray.

In-toeing

Her toes point inwards, which can make her fall over her feet as she walks. This is another common problem and one that corrects itself in most cases. Sometimes the knees point inwards, but this usually improves by itself and most children will be walking normally by 8 years of age.

Occasionally in-toeing is caused by the legs and knees facing forwards and just the front of the feet turning inwards. If this is the case then ensure that your child is properly measured for shoes. Also, see your GP because physiotherapy and stretching exercises can help.

Flat feet

All toddlers have flat feet when they first start to walk. You'll notice that your child stands with her feet wide apart and her ankles rolled inwards. But as the muscles strengthen, your child will walk with her feet closer together and the ankles will straighten. By the time your child can stand on tiptoe in a few months' time, you'll see her arches.

WHAT'S HAPPENING TO MUM AND DAD

A night away can do wonders for a relationship when you've got a toddler. By now your baby is probably in a reasonable sleeping and feeding routine and not waking too often at night, which makes it more likely that grandparents or friends will agree to have her for a night. Your baby should be happy enough if she's left with someone she knows well. And one option is that the person stays in your home while you're away, which means your baby is in familiar surroundings.

You'll be amazed at how luxurious it feels to be alone with your partner – a night together without even the tiniest chance that you'll have to get up for your baby. You'll be able to have a late breakfast, take your time and not worry about hot coffee getting spilled. It's very liberating and restorative for your relationship, probably cheaper than counselling and certainly a lot more fun! You're bound to talk mostly about your baby and miss her desperately, but you'll still relish your time alone with each other.

PLANNING AHEAD

Start building up an 'arts and craft box' for your baby by collecting paper to draw and paint on, pretty pieces of old wrapping paper for sticking, old birthday cards, toilet rolls, egg boxes, cereal packets, feathers, autumn leaves, shells and so on. Your baby won't be old enough to be creative and make things until she is over 2, but in the meantime she will enjoy helping you and rummaging through her craft box.

MONTH 17

INTRODUCTION

Last month we mentioned how toddlers around this age can sometimes be quite aggressive. One of the most unpleasant forms of aggression has to be biting, and any parent of a biter will be familiar with the shame and the stigma you feel.

Although vicious, toddler biting is not premeditated and your child won't actually be trying to hurt anyone. It's an impulsive act because she wants her own way, usually to play with another child's toy, and she's found a way of getting it. Little children may also bite if they are frustrated with an adult.

So what do you do if your little one bites? First, make sure that the child or person she has bitten is OK, and that your child doesn't get rewarded with the toy she 'bit' for. Then take her away from the situation, perhaps sit her on your knee away from other children to calm down. It's important to act instantly and to spell out that biting is wrong, 'We don't bite. Biting hurts.'

Don't shout or lose your temper (not always easy). Biting incidents can get emotional and you don't want to add to this – it's your job to take the heat out of the situation. *Never* bite back – some parents do this to teach their child that biting hurts, but it's actually very confusing because your child is being told not to bite yet you are biting her.

You won't necessarily be able to stop your child biting altogether before she reaches 3 (most biters stop at around this age), but you can learn the signals that she's about to attack. A clenched jaw can be a giveaway, and some children only bite if they're in a large group of children, or if they're particularly tired, hungry, teething or coming down with a cold. Monitor your child closely so that you can intervene before there's an incident.

One of the most difficult things to cope with is other parents and nursery staff. Biting obviously hurts, but serious damage is rarely done. Even so, the reactions from other parents can seem extreme and out of proportion to the situation. Apologize politely but try not to let it get to you. You'll feel like the worst parent in the world, but just remind yourself that small children have always bitten and always will, and that most grow out of it and turn into perfectly reasonable and civilized adults.

As a parent of a biter, the best thing you can do is to remain calm and consistent whenever your child bites. Do find out how your nursery or childminder deals with biting – it may not be age-appropriate. For example, children under about 2½ shouldn't be put on naughty steps because they're too young to understand the link between their behaviour and the punishment.

Likewise, there's no point taking your child home from a play date or playgroup if she bites, although sometimes it can be a relief to escape. But at this age your child doesn't have the understanding or a good enough memory to make the association between biting and being taken home. Also, she won't yet have the language skills to understand what is going on. You need to wait until she is 2½ to 3 before being 'taken home' has any impact.

SLEEP

Aim: uninterrupted night sleep 11–12 hours
To bed early – about 7 or 8 p.m.
One lunchtime nap (1½–2 hours)
A total of 14 hours' sleep

Just about all toddlers will end their morning nap now if they haven't already done so – as we mentioned in Month 9, some babies drop this sleep much earlier.

As for your toddler's longer lunchtime sleep, this will probably last around 2 hours, although sometimes she'll only sleep for an hour and a half, or perhaps less. Some children start to need less sleep at lunchtime from around now, which can be tough if you've been relying on this time slot to catch up and do your own thing.

But if your toddler seems happy to play quietly in her cot for half an hour before she sleeps, this is fine – it's all rest time. Most children need a daytime nap until they are about 3, otherwise they'll become very cranky in the late afternoon. So do keep putting your toddler down for her nap – you may well find that she goes through phases of not sleeping particularly well during the afternoon, then suddenly starts again. This could be for any number of reasons, for example if she's not very active in the morning, or perhaps if she's teething.

Over the next 6 months you may notice that your toddler starts to need less sleep at night, in which case you can cut her daytime nap back to just an hour. Do continue to encourage her daytime nap until she is about 3, because this usually helps night sleep. If children don't have their daytime sleep, they can end up overtired and find it difficult to settle at bedtime – similarly adults can become so exhausted that their brains whirr at night instead of being able to drift calmly off to sleep.

Troubleshooting

Because we live in a flat, our baby still sleeps in our bedroom, in her own cot. How do we have sex without waking her?
Children tend to sleep more deeply during the first half of the night, so before about midnight you can be noisier and probably get away with turning the light on. Having said that, even during the first half of the night children (like adults) sleep in cycles and will sometimes go into a lighter sleep. If your child seems to be rousing, switch the light off and keep quiet for a few minutes and this should be enough time for her to go back into a very deep sleep – you'll notice her breathing deeply as her heart rate slows again.

FEEDING

Fussy eating is notorious among toddlers, and there are many reasons for this. We've noticed that from around now some children go off casseroles, foods with a sauce or anything in which food is mixed up and they can't identify familiar ingredients. It usually helps if you serve your toddler her different foods separately. So rather than giving her a bowl of mixed up spaghetti bolognaise and carrots, you could serve her carrots, pasta and bolognaise sauce side by side on her plate so that she can easily recognize each food.

Make a point of not being too careful when you serve her food, though, or you could end up with your toddler refusing to eat her carrots if they get 'touched' by the bolognaise. For this reason we don't recommend toddler plates that come with sections to separate different foods.

It can also help if you get your toddler involved in preparing her food so that she understands what the strange-looking sauces and so on contain – this obviously works best if she likes and is familiar with the ingredients. Putting your baby in the highchair and letting her watch you cook can work very well. We'll talk more about getting your child involved in cooking in Month 22 – and about refusing foods in Month 23.

DEVELOPMENT AND PLAY

Talking

Most toddlers are vocal but not very verbal at this age, although plenty will start to say 'No' around now – usually within a few months of learning to talk.

This is an easy word to pronounce and it's also an effective way for your toddler to assert her wants. So your conversations may sound something like this: 'Do you want lunch?' 'No.' 'Let's put your shoes on.' 'No.' 'Let's go to the park.' 'No.'

Developmentally it's natural for your toddler to become increasingly independent and assertive, but the 'No' stage can also be infuriating.

Try giving your toddler a choice. At lunchtime, you can say 'Do you want the red plate or the blue plate?' – this allows her to have some control over her world without getting into the 'No' battle. Giving your toddler choices throughout the day will probably have a calming effect and help her to feel more independent and in control – 'This story or that one?', 'The green jumper or the stripy one?' and so on.

As for the park, don't *ask* your toddler, *tell* her by saying something like 'When we go to the park you can go on the swings and go down the slide.' You can be putting her shoes on while telling her this. Hopefully she won't object because she'll be thinking so hard about the park.

MILESTONES

(All babies are different – you probably won't be able to tick everything on this list.)

☐ *Steady on her feet* – once your toddler has been walking for a few months she'll be able to bend over and pick up objects while remaining on her feet, walk up a step and even start to run.

☐ *Rides a toy vehicle* – some children will have the balance and coordination to push themselves along on a toy car or tractor. But at this age they won't get very far.

☐ *Kiss it better* – around now, your toddler will start to find it comforting if you 'kiss it better' whenever she hurts herself.

☐ *Rapidly developing vision* – most babies are long-sighted until they're about 2, and by now this is already improving (most children have 20/20 vision at 3). This means that close activities become easier as your toddler is better able to see objects that are near to hand. So you may notice that she starts to really enjoy books around now and spends time looking at the pictures.

☐ *Throws a ball* – some babies will be able to throw a ball using a clumsy underarm throw. Others won't be able to do this until they are nearly 2. Smallish soft balls are the easiest for babies to hold.

☐ *Turning knobs* – your baby will have the fine motor skills to be able to make the twisting motion to turn knobs as she approaches 18 months. This means that she'll have lots of fun playing with the telly, the radio and the knobs on the stove – so watch out.

☐ *Looks at what you're looking at* – if you look at a cat in the garden and comment, your toddler will now be able to see the direction you are looking in and work out where the cat is.

WHEN TO WORRY

If your baby is not yet pulling herself up to standing, or isn't cruising, this can sometimes indicate a problem with her gross motor skills, so get her checked out.

SAFETY TIP OF THE MONTH

There's no getting away from the fact that toddlers can be infuriating and exhausting, and the temptation to smack your child can sometimes feel overwhelming. Don't give in to this temptation, however, because although it will give you a sense of release and probably stop your toddler doing whatever it was that was infuriating you, it won't improve her behaviour long term. First, you'll be giving her the confusing message that it's OK for Mummy or Daddy to be violent but not OK if she is. Secondly, children under 2 can't make the connection between their behaviour and the smack, because they are too young to understand the difference between right and wrong. And finally, smacking your toddler will encourage her to be aggressive.

But knowing all this in theory doesn't make it any easier in the heat of the moment. Our advice is to accept that you can't reason with a small child, then, as soon as you feel yourself starting to lose control, ensure she is safe and then walk away. Put the kettle on, take some deep breaths and you'll be surprised how quickly you calm down. The trick is to walk away as soon as you start to feel stressed. Otherwise you'll become so worked up that you'll be more likely to shout, scream and hit than have the presence of mind to be able to leave the room. And of course if your partner or anyone else is around, ask them to come and take over when you feel yourself losing it.

No one's saying it's easy, and some toddlers require almost super-human self-control to look after, but as children get older they become even more likely to push your buttons and drive you crazy. So the better you become at learning to calm yourself, the less likely you are to smack your child. And for help with managing stress, you could contact the stress management society at www. stress.org.uk.

WHEN TO SEE THE DOCTOR ✚

Sunburn

From around now your toddler may object to wearing sun cream and a sunhat, and because she's mobile it's impossible to make her stay in the shade. Most children cooperate by the time they're 3 and are able to understand the dangers of sunburn, but in the meantime your toddler is vulnerable and you need ways to protect her. Long trousers and sleeves are easier than plastering limbs with sun cream, and they also give better protection.

For faces, you can try putting sun cream on together – if your toddler sees you putting it on your nose and cheeks she may cooperate, or you could let her rub your cream in and you rub in hers, or perhaps let her put her own cream on. Another trick is to put her cream on quickly and, when she objects, pretend to rub the cream off – obviously you'll actually be rubbing it in.

As for sunhats, choose one with an under-chin strap, as these are more difficult for a toddler to fling off. If she's particularly reluctant about putting a hat on in the first place you could try offering her two hats and letting her choose which she wants to wear – feeling she's got a choice and therefore some control can help.

If your child does burn, give her baby ibuprofen or paracetamol to soothe the pain, which generally eases within 24 hours of the skin being burnt. You could also give her a lukewarm bath, but don't bother with after-sun or other 'soothing' creams because your toddler will find it uncomfortable having these rubbed in and they don't soothe the skin much anyway. Make sure that your child has plenty to drink so that she is rehydrated.

With severe sunburn you'll need to take your child to hospital – look out for the following danger signs: a fever of 38°C or higher, vomiting, deliriousness or febrile fits (a fit caused by a sudden rise in body temperature – see Month 18).

WHAT'S HAPPENING TO MUM AND DAD

It's very common for mums to complain that dads aren't doing enough to help out. The classic advice is to sit down and decide who does what on the domestic front, but chances are you'll end up arguing, and you're unlikely to ever get things completely 'fair'.

So our big tip is to let Dad have sole charge – he'll relish being able to do things his own way, but hopefully realize there's quite a lot involved and be a little more sympathetic in the future.

If you haven't gone back to work, you'll be spending hours with your baby during the week, so at weekends you may well be keen for a break. And if you're working full time, it can be very luxurious to have an hour or two to yourself at weekends – don't feel guilty about spending even more time away from your baby, we're only talking an additional hour or two a week. So persuade your partner to take your baby out, or go out yourself. You'll find it very liberating to have your home to yourself and be able to move from room to room without your toddler making demands. Likewise, if you go out it may feel strange not having the buggy and a list in your head (snack, water, nappy, warm enough) to keep your child happy.

Try to resist giving your partner too many instructions or any criticism, and hopefully you'll get time to yourself on a regular basis, which will do wonders for your tolerance levels. And your partner will love spending time with his toddler – especially if he never gets 'told off'.

PLANNING AHEAD

Once your child starts trying to climb out of her cot (which can happen from as early as next month) she'll need to go into a big bed. It's worth considering your options in case you have to rush out and buy a big bed quickly – although a cot mattress on the floor is fine as a makeshift bed if you haven't had a chance to shop.

There's no need to go shopping if you've got a cot bed – just make sure you have any spare panels to hand that you'll need to convert it from a cot to a bed.

Otherwise you have to decide whether you're going to get a child's bed, a standard single bed or even bunk beds. The advantage of a child's bed is that it will probably be cheaper, and is also smaller so easier for your toddler to get in and out of. This will last until your child is about 6. A single bed, on the other hand, could last until she leaves home and may well be more comfortable. Toddlers do cope with full-sized single beds, although a small step can help them get in and out – also watch out for the height, as some children will fall out of bed at night (more on this in Month 18).

MONTH 18

INTRODUCTION

From around 18 months, toddlers become less impulsive and start to 'stop and think' as their brain develops and cognitive skills improve. If you watch your toddler you will almost certainly be able to see the cogs beginning to turn as she works things out. For example, if she's riding a tractor with a trailer on the back, she may spot a toy that she likes, stop to get it, put it in the trailer and continue to ride. Until now she would probably have got off the tractor and simply gone off to play with the new toy that she'd seen.

As reasoning skills develop you'll notice that your toddler doesn't rush into things as much but thinks a little more. And from around now you'll see early signs of self control – your toddler may be less likely to snatch a toy or push another child off a ride-on car. And if she's sitting in her highchair she may not cry for her lunch to be given to her 'right now' if she can see you serving it up.

Such changes will happen gradually. But if your toddler is particularly lively and energetic, you'll certainly notice that things get a little easier from this age – although there are lots more challenges ahead, so don't relax just yet.

It's interesting to note that children who start to walk late, at about 18 months, won't have so many falls and bumps as early walkers. This is because they are more considered in their approach and more aware of their capabilities.

SLEEP

Aim: uninterrupted night sleep 11–12 hours
To bed early – about 7 or 8 p.m.
One lunchtime nap (1½–2 hours)
A total of 13½ hours' sleep

Big Bed

Most toddlers don't go into a big bed until they are about 2 and are 91cm tall – the height estimated to allow them to climb out of their cots. But as we mentioned last month, your child may need a big bed as early as this month if she is very tall for her age or is particularly adventurous and agile.

Prepare her by talking about big beds, explaining what it will be like. You can use the same bedding to keep it familiar, although you'll need new sheets, of course (your toddler can have a full-sized single duvet at a later stage).

On your toddler's first day in her new bed, try to ensure that she has an active day and so will be tired, then keep the bedtime routine the same as usual.

To stop your toddler falling out of bed you can put a rolled-up towel along the edge of her bed under the sheet. This barrier will remind your child where the edge of the bed is while she sleeps. You can also put a couple of pillows on the floor for the first week or so to break her fall if she slips out of bed. There's no need to spend money on a bed guard – the trouble with these is that parents don't get rid of them and they can stay up needlessly for months.

Lots of parents dread the transition from a cot to a bed because suddenly their baby is no longer contained, which can be challenging both at bedtime and early in the morning. And yes you probably will find that once you've left the room your toddler gets up, simply because she can.

Lead her gently back to bed then say goodnight and leave (you can do the same if she ever gets up in the middle of the night). Be as quick and boring as you can, because if you spend time explaining why she must stay in bed, your toddler will see this as some sort of 'reward' for getting out of bed and will do it again. But if nothing much happens, she'll soon tire of getting up (usually after a few nights) and be happy to stay in her bed. The worst thing you can do is get cross and shout because this will frighten a timid toddler and excite a brave one – but both will be flooded with adrenaline, a stress hormone that will keep your toddler awake for at least another hour.

When it comes to moving to the big bed, mornings can be even more challenging than bedtime because your child won't be tired and is likely to get up at dawn and want to explore the home. This is potentially very dangerous, particularly at this young age. You could keep the bedroom door shut. Set some toys up for her the night before, like a teddy bears' picnic, or build the train set layout. It will take a few minutes but could buy you around 20 minutes in the morning – a pretty good trade-off.

Another option is to allow your toddler into your bed in the mornings – lots of parents do this and it can be fun to have some family time together before getting up. But do be aware that this can become a habit that's difficult to break – and your toddler won't be able to tell the time and may think it's fine to come into your bed if she wakes at 4 a.m.

Your final option is to get up early. While 6 a.m. isn't the ideal time for most people to start the day, if you make the most of those early hours and get your chores done you can have a rest later. And if you work, you could look into starting your work day earlier and then leaving earlier.

Troubleshooting

My child sometimes sweats profusely in her sleep, is this OK?
It's quite common for young children to sweat at night, especially if they're slightly unwell – perhaps with a cold. Do check that your child doesn't have a fever – a temperature above 38°C – and if she does then you can give her Calpol or baby ibuprofen to bring it down.

Otherwise you can change her pyjamas and pillow case – if she's in a deep sleep she may not even wake up (we mentioned sleep cycles in Month 14). If you leave her wet, she may become cold and wake up later anyway.

FEEDING

Iron Deficiency in Bottle-fed Babies

Watch out to see if your toddler is grumpy, tired and listless, doesn't have much appetite but still drinks lots of milk from a bottle. If this is the case, there is a chance that she is iron deficient – in which case you may also notice that she has pale pink lower eyelids instead of bright red ones.

Iron deficiency and anaemia often show up around now if toddlers have been drinking so much milk from a bottle that they aren't eating enough solids, and so are missing out on iron-rich foods such as meat and eggs (See the Meal Planning chapter for more on iron-rich foods).

Because one of the symptoms of anaemia is appetite loss, this perpetuates the problem, so it's important to see your GP. Your GP may refer you to a dietician, who will probably prescribe iron medication. Once your child's iron levels increase, her appetite will also improve.

DEVELOPMENT AND PLAY

Talking – some babies will say their first word around now. This is a bit late, but rarely anything to worry about. It's actually more important that your child understands what is being said to her. If your child still hasn't said a word, then get her checked out – see 'When to Worry', page 175.

If your toddler is able to say single words, she may soon start using repetitive words such as night-night, bye-bye, woof-woof, row-row (the boat), and so on. And she may start to practise inflection around now – for example raising and lowering her tone as she says 'night-night', just as she hears you say it.

MILESTONES

(All babies are different – you probably won't be able to tick everything on this list.)

☐ *Getting faster* – some 18-month-olds will be running quite quickly by now. They may also be able to walk upstairs one at a time while holding your hand, as well as walk backwards and pivot.

☐ *Carrying while walking* – this is a classic 18-month milestone. Toddlers have the coordination to be able to carry toys and other objects while they walk.

☐ *Getting on a chair* – your toddler may be able to climb onto a chair and position herself correctly. She'll find this easier with child-sized chairs, but watch out as these can be very light and topple over easily.

☐ *Dancing* – once your child is steady on her feet, she will love dancing. Young children have a natural rhythm, so turn on the music and have fun – she will love moving in time to the music. This is a good age to join a singing or music group with her.

☐ *Scribbling with crayons* – your toddler probably has the fine motor skills to use a crayon and even a pen. So give her lots of paper and pens to play with. She'll love it if you draw something she recognizes such as a face or a cat. She probably won't want to draw for more than a few minutes at a time at this age.

☐ *Kicking a ball* – if your toddler was an early walker she may be able to kick a ball by now. Find a very light ball, as she won't be able to kick very hard. Lots of children can't kick balls until they are about 2.

☐ *Stops the 'overlap' grasp* – pass your baby a cup and she may start cupping it in her hand instead of putting her fingers or thumb inside it to pick it up.

☐ *Left- or right-handed* – you may see whether your baby is going to be left- or right-handed around now. Before this she would have been completely ambidextrous.

☐ *Nose-picking* – children start to pick their noses and often eat it from the age of around 18 months. As they become socially aware they will stop picking their nose so publicly.

☐ *Putting things in the bin* – this can start from around now and your child will simply be having a fun game of posting things. She may also post things through floorboards or your letter box, and will of course be oblivious to the havoc she causes as keys and credit cards disappear. It's quicker and easier to keep important things out of reach than to teach her not to 'post'.

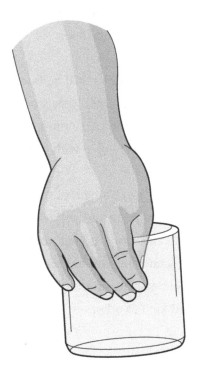

Your baby will stop putting her fingers or thumb inside a cup when she wants to pick it up, but will instead cup her hands around it.

☐ *Fitting things inside* – at this age your child will enjoy simple puzzles and toys where she fits a shape into a shape box.

☐ *Wanting to use tools* – your toddler will be fascinated with tools around now and will want to use keys, phones, mascara (boys, too!), brooms and anything that she sees you using to carry out a task. You can give her old keys, toy phones and toy brooms to play with – she'll love copying you.

☐ *Showing you things* – there's an element of cause-and-effect in this gesture as your toddler gives you something and you react by being pleased. But the interesting developmental milestone is that your toddler is showing signs that she not only understands that you are separate from her, but also that you too have feelings – in this case, interest in her toy. This is an early stage of being sympathetic and kind to others.

WHEN TO WORRY

Walking

If your baby still isn't walking, then it's worth getting her checked out because there may be a developmental problem – the sooner this is identified, the better. However, if she's a bottom-shuffler then you almost certainly don't need to worry if she's still not walking. The reason is that bottom shufflers have the advantage over crawlers in that they can look up as they move, and also carry things. But being able to do this makes them less motivated to get up and walk, unlike crawlers who are more driven – they get fed up only being able to look down as they move, and not being able to carry things easily. Lots of bottom-shufflers don't walk until they are 2.

Talking

If your toddler still hasn't said a word, then take her to the doctor, who may refer her for a speech therapy assessment. She will probably be monitored until she is 2, then, depending on her progress, she may or may not need speech therapy.

Some children speak late for no apparent reason, just as some children are late walkers – it could be linked with genetics and how the brain develops, nobody really knows for sure. It is worth getting your child assessed, though, because if she needs professional help with her talking, then having some speech therapy will stop her falling too far behind. This will benefit her later on with things like socializing with other children, potty-training and learning colours and numbers.

Speech therapy stigma

Because the home environment has a big impact on speech development, some parents feel a bit ashamed if their child needs speech therapy. But it certainly doesn't always follow that your child has delayed speech because you haven't spent enough time talking and responding to her.

Any good speech therapist will be well aware that plenty of children in 'non-stimulating environments' do very well with their speech, and also lots of children in 'stimulating environments' have delayed speech. So don't let any perceived stigma put you off seeking help and doing what is best for your child.

SAFETY TIP OF THE MONTH

We've mentioned climbing out of cots and big beds this month. But even if your child isn't trying to climb out of her cot yet, get into the habit of clearing away any sharp toys left near the cot so that there's nothing nasty for her to fall on. The first time a child climbs out of her cot nearly always takes parents by surprise. And if your child is making a fuss to come out of her cot, don't ignore her in case she flings herself out in a rage.

WHEN TO SEE THE DOCTOR ✚

Febrile fits

These can occur from 6 months, although they are increasingly more likely from around now. They affect up to 5 per cent of children until the age of 6. The fit can happen if your baby's temperature rises very suddenly, causing your baby to lose consciousness, with symptoms including eyes rolling and her body going stiff and jerking. The fit will be short and stop by itself, and afterwards your baby will be sleepy.

If your child starts fitting, call 999 for an ambulance then lie your child on the floor on her side, checking that she's not choking on dribble or vomit. Don't try to restrain her, but stroke her gently and talk in a soothing voice. Cuddling her close will stop her from losing heat, so don't do this even after the fit has stopped.

Time the length of the fit (using a watch or clock with a second hand) and observe closely to see if her whole body is fitting or if the fit began on just one side – your doctor will ask questions about this later.

Afterwards your baby may be very sleepy and hard to rouse, then wake after about 5 minutes before falling asleep again. To bring your baby's temperature down you can cool her with a tepid sponge, remove excess clothing and take her away from any hot radiators. The idea is to let her cool gently, so don't be tempted to strip her naked and put her in a freezing bath. You can also give her baby paracetamol (Calpol) and/or baby ibuprofen if she's not had any in the last 4 hours.

Your doctor will eliminate meningitis and a urinary tract infection. If your baby is clear of these illnesses then there is no risk from further problems, although she will be more prone to having fits in the future.

A febrile fit can be a trigger for epilepsy if your child has a predisposition to this condition, but the fit is not a cause of epilepsy in itself.

WHAT'S HAPPENING TO MUM AND DAD

Something that working couples of young children have to decide is who stays at home to look after your child when she's ill. If your child goes to nursery or has a childminder, one of you will definitely have to take time off, but if she's with grandparents or a nanny then you probably won't. You may also need time off if your carer becomes ill.

Often, it automatically becomes Mum's role to take time off. If this works for your family, then don't change anything – there's no point trying to make things 'fair' if it's actually impractical, just for the sake of it. But do bear in mind that if you're taking time off as paid holiday you only have a certain entitlement a year – and there's no point in one of you using all your holiday up while the other stores up a large bank of days off. It's more practical to share so that you both still have plenty of days to take off together as a family.

You'll also need to work out who is going to be able to take time off work more easily. If, say, Mum is under threat of redundancy or has a nightmare boss, then it may make sense for Dad to take the time off to look after your sick baby. Or perhaps one of you has a desperately important meeting that could sway things towards a promotion in the near future.

Just bear in mind that this is a particularly sticky point for most couples. You're already under pressure if you're both working and bringing up a baby, and suddenly you are faced with extra stress.

As with most things related to childcare, it's a case of muddling through the unknown and working things out as you go along.

You can also look at parental leave (see Month 19). This offers a few more options and can work well if your child has a serious or long-term illness.

PLANNING AHEAD

Book a family holiday, or visit family who live abroad, because flights for the under-2s are usually free (although there's no baggage allowance). Once your toddler turns 2 you'll be landed with having to pay your child's fare which is around 50 per cent of the adult price or more.

Of course flying with a small child can be challenging – sometimes very challenging indeed – but it will be a few years yet before it gets much easier, so you may as well make the most of not having to pay.

MONTH 19

INTRODUCTION

From around now your toddler will look less like a rounded, cuddly baby and more like a small child because her limbs and neck will lengthen, she'll lose more of her baby fat, and her muscles will develop. You'll also notice that her movements become quicker and smoother, which again is more like a child than a baby.

This is also the age when children can start to get frightened by things – typically happening from 18 months to about 2 years. So your toddler may become very upset by the vacuum cleaner, dogs, toilets or even sirens.

Being scared can help protect us from danger, and toddler fears are a normal developmental milestone. You'll see that over the next 6 months or so your child will gradually become less anxious about everyday things as they become familiar and she understands them.

In the meantime you can help your toddler by putting yourself in her shoes – imagine that you're with your partner and an 8-foot monster walks into the room. You'd be terrified, and if your partner told you not to be silly and that the monster wouldn't hurt you, you'd still be terrified. And if your partner teased you, you'd probably become hysterical because it would feel as though he was taking sides with the monster and not you.

But what if your partner gave you lots of comfort, and perhaps led you away from the monster so that you could peep at it from a distance while your partner went over to 'chat' to it? This would ease your fears a little – especially if your partner remained calm and relaxed.

The other thing that would help would be if your partner told you whenever the monster was about to come back again – this would eliminate any surprises. But you'd need to see the monster several times before you even began to relax. And it would probably take months until you stopped being afraid.

For your toddler, a vacuum cleaner, a toilet, a dog or anything she's scared of is a 'monster'. So be patient and help her get over her fears in her own time.

Lots of parents unwittingly pass on their own phobias to their children, so however much you may dislike dogs, spiders or perhaps mice, try to disguise your feelings. And when it comes to dogs, do ask the owner if the dog is OK with children before going ahead and showing your child how to close her fist for the dog to sniff and then helping her to pat the dog. It's also important to explain to your child when she isn't allowed to touch a dog – perhaps saying 'This dog isn't used to children and may bite; let's find a friendly dog for you to pat.'

SLEEP

Aim: uninterrupted night sleep 11–12 hours
To bed early – about 7 or 8 p.m.
One lunchtime nap (1½–2 hours)
A total of 13½ hours' sleep

Some families choose not to follow the conventional toddler sleep pattern of early nights and an afternoon nap. If this works for you, that's fine – plenty of cultures think nothing of having young children around in the evenings.

But do ensure that your child is getting enough sleep – when children get very tired, adrenaline (a stress hormone) can kick in and this gives them loads of wild energy and they don't seem sleepy at all.

Try this quiz to see if your child needs more sleep:

☐ Sometimes she falls asleep over an hour earlier than her usual bedtime.

☐ You have to wake her most mornings.

☐ She falls asleep nearly every time she goes out in the car.

☐ She falls asleep nearly every time she goes in the buggy.

☐ She seems very tired during the day and cries easily.

If you ticked one or more of the above, then do reassess your child's sleep patterns. At this age she needs at least 13 hours' sleep, preferably 13½, in 24 hours (her night sleep and naps combined).

Troubleshooting

Is it OK for my toddler to sleep in the pitch dark?
Unless your toddler doesn't like the dark, continue to shut her door at bedtime, because this is a clear signal that it's time to go to sleep. Also, our bodies release the sleep hormone melatonin when it's dark, but light suppresses this hormone. So your toddler will feel naturally sleepier in the dark.

As soon as she starts to object, give her a night light or leave her door open a little. Fear of the dark can begin any time from now until the age of about 2½.

FEEDING

Tooth Decay

If your baby still comfort-sucks on a bottle or baby cup of milk, squash or fruit juice, particularly at night, then she may have tooth decay. Even comfort-sucking on the breast can cause decay.

Take her to the dentist for a check-up. It's especially important that your child sees a dentist if you notice brown marks on her teeth, which are probably cavities. Although children this age are too young to cooperate with routine dental check-ups, if there is a problem your dentist will somehow manage to check her teeth and may refer her for a hospital dental appointment to have teeth taken out under a general anaesthetic.

Don't get too alarmed, though – it's fine for your toddler to drink milk, and also dilute fruit juice occasionally, either with meals or if she's thirsty. It is the clinging to the cup or bottle and constant sipping which causes problems. Sipping water is OK, too, although children are unlikely to comfort-suck on water because it isn't sweet.

If your child doesn't comfort-suck on milk or juice, she's unlikely to have decay at this age. But it's not too soon to start getting her used to the dentist: simply take her along when you have an appointment – although leave her behind if you need any serious treatment done, or if you happen to be nervous about the dentist. You don't want to put her off.

When it comes to brushing, your child may be an expert at clamping her mouth shut, which is a worry as she will probably have most of her teeth by now. Providing you stay relaxed, children are likely to cooperate with teeth cleaning from around the age of 2.

In the meantime, continue to get the brush out a couple of times a day and either let your toddler brush her own teeth or, if she lets you, have a quick brush yourself. In our experience you'll be lucky to be allowed to brush her teeth for more than a few seconds every few days. But this isn't a problem if you limit the sugar and sweet drinks in your child's diet (see Month 20).

You can try using a little baby toothpaste – most toddlers like the taste, and this can help persuade them to cooperate. But you'll need to hide it to stop them eating half the tube. Also hide your own toothpaste to ensure your child doesn't eat it. If swallowed, the high fluoride content in adult paste can cause fluorosis – harmless white marks on the teeth.

DEVELOPMENT AND PLAY

Talking

Even if your toddler is able to say some words by now, she may sometimes chatter away in a gobbledegook language as she practises the rhythm and intonation of sentences. You can encourage this very charming phase by giving her a toy telephone, or simply chattering back in a 'made up' language.

Early talkers may start putting two words together around now. For example, 'like dog' means 'I like that dog', and 'Tom nana' means 'I (Tom) want a banana.' Some babies won't put two words together until they are about 2; this is completely normal.

MILESTONES

(All babies are different – you probably won't be able to tick everything on this list.)

☐ *Runs away* – once your toddler is able to run she'll have great fun escaping from you and will see this as an exciting game. She'll be particularly tempted to run when she sees long straight aisles – supermarkets, churches and hotel corridors will be delightfully tempting for the runaway toddler.

☐ *Won't hold hands* – once your toddler has learned to walk at a reasonable pace, you may take her out for short walks. But lots of toddlers object to holding hands. This may be because you are walking too fast, not stopping for enough breaks or perhaps holding your toddler's arm at an uncomfortably high angle. Or perhaps she is simply so delighted to be free of her buggy that she resents the restriction of having to hold hands. This is fine in the park, but a problem on the pavement. You could try reins – held loosely, these give a feeling of independence. You can also get wrist bands, although if your child won't hold hands she'll probably object to wearing one of these. But at this age it's often easier to keep your child in the buggy until you reach somewhere safe like a park.

☐ *Has tantrums* – we've all heard of the terrible 2s, but most children have their first tantrum well before this age. Tantrums generally occur when you try and stop your child doing what she wants, and at this age she will cry loudly and refuse to cooperate. (Lying down on the pavement comes later.) We cover tantrums in more detail in Month 21.

☐ *Fights hair-washing* – this happens partly because your toddler dislikes having water and shampoo in her eyes, and also because she's trying to assert herself and is now agile enough to resist hair-washing effectively. Most children become more cooperative after their second birthday, but in the meantime you could rinse her hair with water and only use shampoo occasionally. Children's hair doesn't get greasy in the way an adult's does, so it's more a matter of washing food out from time to time after a particularly sticky meal.

☐ *Checks your reaction* – if something unfamiliar happens, such as a balloon bursting or a dog growling, your toddler may look at your face to check your reaction. If you appear upset, she will feel frightened. Likewise, if you remain relaxed and happy, this will help your toddler remain calm.

☐ *Becomes aware that she's doing a wee or poo* – somewhere between 18 months and 2 years, most children develop an awareness that they are going to the toilet – this is likely to be a few months earlier for girls than boys. Your child may start telling you that she's doing a poo, or perhaps stop playing and squat. Most children don't start potty-training until after the age of 2, but you can start preparing your child. The best way is to let her watch you go to the toilet, and once she's good at climbing you could even let her climb onto the toilet (lid down) and flush it. This will help her not to be afraid of the toilet when the time eventually comes for her to start sitting on it. There's no point in pushing toilet training too soon, or you may put your child off.

WHEN TO WORRY

If your toddler sits very close to the television it can indicate a vision or hearing problem. Having said that, many young toddlers find it easier to concentrate on the television if they sit close. So look out for signs that she consistently doesn't see or hear what you expect her to. It's always worth being aware of your child's vision and hearing, because problems can occasionally develop over time, even in children who previously had no problems.

Also, if your toddler can't point to one or two body parts such as her eyes and tummy, despite your efforts to teach her, it may be worth asking your doctor to check her development.

And, if she can't turn the pages of a cardboard book, it may indicate problems with her motor skills.

SAFETY TIP OF THE MONTH ⓘ

Drawn to danger

By the time your child is 19 months old she'll be fairly bored with any cupboards and drawers that she's familiar with. Even playing with doors will be a bit dull by now. So she'll be on the lookout for new things to explore, and will no doubt pounce on anything that's left lying around, such as a tool box, a visitor's handbag, a sewing kit or a bag of shopping. You'll have to be more alert than ever because your toddler not only moves quickly, but she'll be able to open boxes and bags quickly, too. The ideal solution is obviously that you don't leave things lying around in the first place.

WHEN TO SEE THE DOCTOR ✚

Meningitis

We mentioned meningitis in our last book, *Your Baby Week by Week*. But now your toddler is 19 months, her fontanelle on the top of her head is likely to have completely closed so the symptoms will be different – more like the symptoms an adult would have.

When your child was a few months old she would have been given immunizations against pneumococcus and Haemophilus influenzae Type B (Hib), plus the pneumococcal jab and the meningitis C vaccine. But this won't protect her against all types of meningitis or septicaemia (blood poisoning, which can be caused by the same bacteria that causes meningitis), so you need to know the symptoms because your child can become seriously ill within hours.

Symptoms include a fever, vomiting and irritability – these can also indicate a common cold, making meningitis difficult to spot. So you'll also need to look out for your child having a severe headache, a stiff neck, dislike of bright lights, being very sleepy or difficult to wake, confused or delirious, or having seizures or a rash.

If your child has just one or two of these symptoms and your instincts tell you she's ill, take her to the hospital Emergency Department where doctors will willingly check her and hopefully give her the all-clear.

Don't delay going to hospital, because meningitis can kill within hours, so don't wait around for conclusive symptoms. And if you're sent home and your child becomes worse, go back again – doctors really won't mind checking your child.

If they suspect meningitis, doctors will do a lumbar puncture and your child will be given antibiotics in the back of her hand as a precaution while the doctors wait for the lumbar puncture results.

Bacterial meningitis requires a prolonged course of antibiotics and it can take a couple of months for your baby to recover fully. She will be given a hearing test to rule out deafness. Other complications, including cerebral palsy and learning difficulties, will hopefully be ruled out in time.

The Meningitis Research Foundation has a free 24-hour helpline 080 8800 3344, or visit www.meningitis.org.

WHAT'S HAPPENING TO MUM AND DAD

We mentioned parental leave last month, which gives both parents the right to take unpaid time off work to look after their child. If you have been with your employer for a year or more, you are entitled to take 13 weeks off work before your child is 5 (parents get 13 weeks each). You have to take the leave as weeks rather than days, and you mustn't take longer than four weeks in a year for any one child. Parents of disabled children can take 18 weeks off before your child is 18.

Parental leave can be taken for anything concerning your child's welfare. So, for example, you may need time off to look at schools, settle her into new childcare arrangements, take her to see grandparents, accompany her during a stay in hospital or simply spend more time with her in the early years.

PLANNING AHEAD

Collect your toddler's Bookstart pack. The Bookstart scheme provides free books for all babies, toddlers and children under 4, and aims to get all children to love books. You are now due for your second pack, 18–30 months, which focuses on building language and listening skills. This includes two books, a colouring book, crayons and a nylon satchel and stickers. You can get it from your health visitor at baby clinic, or your local library. Visit www.bookstart. org.uk for more information.

MONTH **20**

INTRODUCTION

In an ideal world, babies wouldn't watch television before the age of at least 2. There's plenty of research showing how it can hinder speech, social development and play. And it's been shown that toddlers don't concentrate for so long on a particular activity if there is background television on.

In the USA and Australia, paediatricians have recommended a ban on television for the under-2s. And a study at Johns Hopkins University found that toddlers who watch over 2 hours a day are more likely to suffer from behavioural problems.

But although we don't advocate television for the under-2s, the reality is that your child has almost certainly started to enjoy television by now. And we know from experience the relief of being able to put a small child in front of the telly for half an hour while you prepare dinner, make a phone call or just have a break.

So what we'd suggest is that you try to stick to a few realistic guidelines. Limit television to 30 minutes a day or less – watching lots of telly has been linked with obesity in children because they aren't as active. And don't let your child watch television within an hour of going to bed – the artificial light from the television is known to reduce levels of the sleep hormone melatonin, and this could affect how easily your toddler gets to sleep.

Finally, try to make television part of your daily routine rather than switching it on randomly when things start getting chaotic. This way, you will stay in charge of what and when your child watches. Otherwise your child will be 'rewarded' by television whenever her behaviour causes upset and Mum 'needs' to plonk her in front of the telly for a while.

As for what your child watches, children's programmes and DVDs targeted at the under-2s are obviously a better choice than adult daytime telly or cartoons aimed at older children.

SLEEP

Aim: uninterrupted night sleep 11–12 hours
To bed early – about 7 or 8 p.m.
One lunchtime nap (1½–2 hours)
A total of 13 hours' sleep

Co-sleeping with your baby isn't recommended by doctors because of concerns about cot death. However, plenty of parents ignore this advice and sleep with their children anyway. Perhaps your toddler was a terrible sleeper as a baby, so you popped her into bed with you and you've never quite broken the habit. If you're a single mum you may find that the burden of having to get up in the night to soothe your child just too much, especially if you're working. So you put her in your bed to ensure you get enough sleep. Or maybe this time-tested sleeping arrangement, which dates back to when time began, simply feels right for you and your family.

Whatever your reasons, there may come a day when you've had enough and want to get your child out of your bed and into her own. The first step is to eliminate all night-feeds if you haven't done so already – even if you don't want to move your child out of your bed you should try to stop night-feeds because of the risk of obesity and tooth decay (even from breastmilk).

If you haven't yet got a bed for your toddler, you can make a big deal about getting a new one. Chances are your child will be enthusiastic and excited about her new bed, and keen to sleep in it. For an existing bed, you could buy some new bedding to make her bed seem special and get her interested.

Explain to your toddler what's going to happen, and perhaps go and see some of her toddler friends' beds – saying something like 'You can sleep in your own big-girl bed, just like Nina' can certainly help.

Then ask your toddler 'Do you want to sleep in your big bed tonight?' If the answer is 'No' accept this and don't push or she'll feel pressurized. Then ask again in about a week. It may take a few weeks before you get a 'Yes' but eventually she'll come round to wanting to sleep in her own bed. The key is to leave off the pressure and let it be her decision.

Once she's sleeping in her new bed, she may become bored or worried and want the comfort of your bed once again. And lots of children who have always happily settled in their own beds will want to get into bed with Mum and Dad from time to time. To stop this becoming a habit, lead your child gently back to her own bed, give her comfort but keep it very boring. Minimize talking and don't offer songs or stories, because if she's 'rewarded' for waking you up she'll do it again.

You'll probably have to repeat this process dozens of times before she gets the message, but it will be worth the effort because when you've cracked it you'll have hours of deep, uninterrupted sleep. Lots of mums describe how they only go into a half-sleep when bed-sharing with their baby and are always aware of their baby being in the bed. This may be nature working its magic as a safety mechanism, but when you are finally free to sleep selfishly with no responsibilities it is truly liberating.

Troubleshooting

We love sharing our bed with our child, but should we stop when our next baby is born?

Because of the link with cot death, we have to advise not bed-sharing with your new baby. But if you plan to go ahead anyway, then it's important to ensure that your older child doesn't sleep next to the new baby. So if you're breastfeeding the baby, then perhaps your older child could sleep next to Dad, away from you and the baby. And if you decide you want your toddler out of your bed when the baby arrives, get her used to her own bed well before the baby comes or she'll think she's been kicked out because you love the baby more than her.

FEEDING

We mentioned last month that toddlers don't cooperate when it comes to brushing teeth. However, if you watch your child's sugar intake this isn't a problem. You need to know that when it comes to tooth care, it's not the amount of sugar that you eat or drink that counts so much as the *frequency*. Our teeth can sustain three acid attacks a day, so it's essential that you limit the times your toddler has sugar – it's much better if she eats a biscuit in one go than lots of mini-biscuits over a longer period of time.

Sugar causes the pH in our mouths to drop from a neutral state to acidic, and when the pH is below 5.5, tooth erosion begins.

As well as sugary foods, the other cause of acidity in our mouths is drinking acidic drinks such as fruit juice. So as well as limiting sugary foods, you also need to limit drinks such as fruit juice and squash.

The most tooth-friendly drink is water, which isn't acidic (has a pH of 7.8) and so doesn't cause an acid attack, and of course contains no sugar.

Milk is also quite tooth-friendly in that it has a pH of 6.5, which again won't cause an acid attack. But as we've said in previous months, milk contains milk sugars, which can damage teeth if your child comfort-sucks from a bottle.

Drinks to be particularly wary of are pure fruit juices such as orange and apple juice (pH 4.1 and 3.5 respectively). Ideally these shouldn't be given to your child at all – whole fruit is much better. But if you do give your toddler fruit juice, dilute it a lot with water and try to give it at the same time as other sweet foods such as biscuits or yoghurts, to minimize the total number of acid attacks.

Sweet fizzy drinks are the worst culprits. Cola has a pH of 2.2, plus lots of sugar, which will of course be very damaging to teeth.

DEVELOPMENT AND PLAY

Talking

A great way to encourage speech is by 'labelling' things. This works well with picture books, so you can say, 'Where's the boat?' and let your toddler touch the picture of the boat. And with story books you can talk about the pictures together as well as reading.

'Please' and 'thank you' – it's never too early to start teaching your baby good manners, and she can certainly learn to say 'please' and 'thank you'. She's too young for you to insist that she says them, but if she hears them often enough she may surprise you one day.

MILESTONES

(All babies are different – you probably won't be able to tick everything on this list.)

☐ *Jumping* – some children will be able to jump on the spot around now, and also jump down from a step.

☐ *Doesn't want to wear a bib* – toddlers can go off bibs at around this age and start to make a lot more fuss if you wipe their faces. Just wipe your toddler's face once at the end of the meal, and dab rather than wipe because wiping the chin triggers saliva production. With bibs, you can try different styles or even a large napkin, or simply use an old t-shirt over clean clothes – if you put it on her 5 minutes before the meal she won't even realize it is a bib. And for summer teatimes, you can take all your toddler's clothes off apart from her nappy, then pop her straight in the bath when she's finished!

☐ *Fascinated by the toilet* – your toddler may discover what fun it is playing with the toilet around now – cleaning it with the toilet brush, flushing it and pulling the toilet paper off the roll. Yes, it's a nuisance, but it's also quite funny and this phase doesn't last long. Wash her hands well afterwards.

☐ *Counting* – your child will mimic counting if she hears it often enough, although she won't understand the concept of numbers until she's about 2½.

☐ *Less aggressive* – some children will start to show a little control and not lash out quite so readily. Although, if they are provoked, children will continue to hit and bite until at least age 3, and often older.

☐ *Resetting things* – toddlers this age will spend lots of time pressing buttons and fiddling. So keep an eye on everything from washing machines and tumble driers to cookers and even cat flaps, or you could end up accidently washing your delicates on a very hot wash, or facing a miserable, wet cat who's been locked out all night.

WHEN TO WORRY

We mentioned pointing things out back in Month 16. If your child still isn't pointing out things that interest her — aeroplanes in the sky, dogs and cats on the street, police cars and so on — it can sometimes indicate autism. Pointing things out shows awareness of others and communication skills, so see your doctor if your child still isn't pointing.

SAFETY TIP OF THE MONTH (i)

Children can fall out of highchairs — this is quite common at this age because your toddler will be agile enough to wriggle in her seat to stand up. Also, she'll probably be resisting any highchair straps by now, so you may well have stopped strapping her in. Keep mealtimes short and when your toddler becomes impatient and fidgety, get her down before she starts standing up. And try and get organized before the meal so that you're not rushing around the kitchen bringing drinks, extra cutlery, cloths to wipe up spills and so on — all the while not watching your child. Ideally sit and relax with your toddler while she eats, and if you need to go and get something, then strap her in — if you're only using the straps occasionally she probably won't resist too much. It goes without saying that you shouldn't leave the room when your toddler is in her highchair, particularly at the end of the meal when she'll be getting fidgety.

WHEN TO SEE THE DOCTOR ✚

Slapped cheeks syndrome

A virus called parvovirus B19 can make children feel unwell for a few days, with a mild fever and then a rash of red spots developing on the cheeks and spreading to the back and tummy. You can treat the fever with Calpol and baby ibuprofen, and you can cool the cheeks with a cool flannel.

The rash can come and go for up to 6 weeks after recovery – triggered by stress, sunlight or when your child gets hot. The virus is easily spread and can cause epidemics in nurseries, although 25 per cent of people who catch it have no symptoms, and around 60 per cent of adults are thought to be immune because they have already had the virus.

Once your child has the rash, she is no longer infectious. But think back about whom your child has been contact with in the 2 weeks before the rash appeared, because pregnant women who catch the virus can have a slightly higher risk of miscarriage if they haven't had the virus before.

If your child gets 'slapped cheek syndrome' there's no need to take her to the doctor unless she seems particularly ill and you're concerned – for example if her fever goes above 39°C and you can't bring it down with Calpol, or if she doesn't want to drink and you're worried about dehydration.

WHAT'S HAPPENING TO MUM AND DAD

Some couples start to get concerned around now if they can't get pregnant again. Secondary infertility is a common yet rarely spoken about issue. You don't get much sympathy because people will often think, 'Surely one child is enough.' Yet the longing for a second child can be very painful – especially when your friends with toddlers start to get pregnant.

If you're over 35, doctors recommend that you seek help after you've been trying to conceive for 6 months. If you're younger, you are advised to try for a year before you seek medical advice. Couples with secondary infertility are often slower to seek help than those who can't conceive first time around. But time may not be on your side, especially if you started your family later.

If it takes longer than planned to get pregnant again, try not to become fixated on having the perfect age gap between your children – there really isn't any such thing. It may sound a bit cheesy, but treasure what you have – you're a mum (or a dad), and you're a family (families come in all sizes). Relish the close bond and the connection that you have with your child – if and when number two comes along, it will be wonderful, but it will also be different.

PLANNING AHEAD

Up until now, if you took your child to a restaurant at lunchtime she may have slept in her buggy. Now she's more likely to remain awake throughout lunch, so you'll need to think ahead. You can check how child-friendly the restaurant is – do they have highchairs or children's activities? Some places provide colouring kits, toys and books or even a special play area. If they don't, then take your own toys. It's also worth having a small snack that your child can eat while you wait to be served – toddlers hate waiting. And pack your toddler's cup with a lid, then she can drink without help while you eat.

MONTH 21

INTRODUCTION

Despite the 'terrible 2s' being notorious for temper tantrums, lots of children start to throw tantrums well before their second birthday. It's worth understanding a bit about tantrums, because this makes them easier to manage. The trigger is usually that your toddler feels frustrated because she can't have what she wants. It could be something as simple as she's balancing along a wall following some older children, and you need her to turn back and go home for lunch.

She will feel so frustrated that the rage system in her primitive (lower) brain will be strongly activated. Her higher brain isn't yet developed enough to override her feelings, and she'll feel genuinely distressed. If you can help her to calm down, it will help her brain development and teach her to soothe feelings of rage and distress in later life.

Distraction can work well to stop a tantrum, because it activates the 'seeking system' in the primitive (or lower) brain and makes the child feel curious and interested. Because the seeking system is in the lower brain, it can easily override the brain's rage or distress systems. It also triggers high levels of the hormone dopamine, which reduces stress and calms your child. So try saying 'Can you see the bird on that tree?' – or anything that you think will interest your child.

It's always worth trying to stop the tantrum occurring in the first place by explaining why your child can't have her own way. So with the walking along the wall scenario, you could try 'We're going on the wall this way to go home for lunch, but the other children live in that direction and have to go on the wall the other way. Let's wave goodbye.'

And of course you can try to soothe your toddler with cuddles, although you may find this seems to upset her further, in which case, continue trying to distract her. If you're desperate, keep a balloon in your pocket and start blowing it up – this simple technique helps most toddlers quickly forget their worries.

SLEEP

Aim: uninterrupted night sleep 11–12 hours
To bed early – about 7 or 8 p.m.
One lunchtime nap (1½–2 hours)
A total of 13 hours' sleep

A milky drink at bedtime has traditionally been used to help sleep. The reason is that milk has a low glycaemic index and is known to release energy slowly, helping you to feel full for longer. So if your toddler still drinks a cup of milk after her dinner, this will certainly help her to sleep.

If she's gone off milk for some reason, or doesn't have a big drink of milk at bedtime, there are plenty of other foods which will help sleep. Other foods that have a low glycaemic index include: yoghurt, apples, peaches, plums, dried apricots, pasta, sweet potatoes and peanut butter. So if you include one or two of these foods in your child's last meal of the day, it may help her to sleep.

Lentils, chickpeas and other pulses also have a very low glycaemic index and can be good bedtime foods. But they can cause wind, so keep portions moderate – servings should about the size of your child's hand.

Troubleshooting

My toddler sleeps quite erratically, how can I get her sleeping more regularly?

Although plenty of parents claim that their toddler sleeps well at night, the reality is often that they don't sleep well *every* night. It's very common for small children to wake in the night from time to time, and it's usually for a good reason such as illness or teething. Also, lots of children's sleep patterns vary slightly from night to night – sometimes they will wake an hour earlier than usual for no apparent reason, at other times they won't settle well at bedtime. If these are one-off instances then don't worry, as this is very common and also normal. Just tighten up your routine for a couple of days to ensure that your child doesn't slip into bad sleeping habits.

FEEDING

Boredom can be a big issue when it comes to feeding toddlers, and if your child is particularly lively she may see food as an interruption to playing and having fun. We recommend a very hands-off, relaxed approach to eating, but some toddlers need a little extra encouragement at around this age and they may stop eating when they are bored rather than when they are full.

The best thing you can do is to eat with your child, ideally having identical food. There's something quite primeval and bonding about sharing a meal, and it really does have a calming effect on children.

Your little one will love the fact that you are eating a boiled egg and soldiers just like her, and will be intrigued as you take the top off your egg and dip your bread in. And if you serve it with some salad or vegetables, she may even try some if she sees you eating them.

The next best thing you can do is to sit down with your toddler while she eats. Even if you're just having a cup of tea, try to eat a little of what she's having – particularly any of the fruit and vegetables. A few beans or tomatoes in between your own meals won't pile on the pounds or spoil your appetite.

Although it's tempting, try to resist tidying the kitchen or getting the washing-up done while your toddler eats – when you're distracted she's more likely to mess about to regain your attention. And if she's a particularly slow eater, then sitting down with her for just some of the time is better than nothing.

It's also a good idea to try to keep meals short – about 20 or 30 minutes is long enough. The key is to ensure that your child is hungry, then she will eat more quickly.

You can also make eating more fun – here are some ideas:

- Find a children's recipe book – lots of them show you how to make hedgehogs, snowmen and funny faces out of food.
- Bite holes in spinach and lettuce leaves 'like a caterpillar'. This will get your toddler's attention and perhaps persuade her to bite a hole herself and start tasting salad leaves.
- Find different, 'grown-up' cutlery. So if your toddler has only used a plastic spoon, give her a metal teaspoon, then another time you can give her a dessert spoon. You can also get children's knives and forks – your child is still too young to use these properly, but if you stick a small piece of food onto her fork she may enjoy popping it into her mouth, just like an adult. And chopsticks can be intriguing to toddlers – of course your toddler won't be able to eat with them very successfully yet, but you can try feeding her little pieces of food from chopsticks. And she'll love watching you eat with chopsticks.
- Have a picnic. Eating outside in the garden or at your local park can be fun. And in the winter you can still have an indoor picnic – put a rug on the floor and invite some teddy bears.

DEVELOPMENT AND PLAY

Talking

Some children start to hum and sing at around this age, and if you've been singing nursery rhymes with your toddler she may have memorized one or two by now. You can encourage this by getting her to fill in the last word of a line. So sing to her, 'Twinkle twinkle little ****,' and see if she is able to say 'star'. This is a fun way to help her learn words.

Some children get in a muddle when answering questions. For example, if you ask your child whether she wants the blue car or the green one, she'll quickly point to what she wants. But if she can't see the cars and you ask her, she'll say 'the green one'. This has little to do with her choice but more to do with her repeating the last thing she heard. As far as she's concerned, she is simply answering a question in the correct way, and will continue to give the 'last' choice that she hears until she is about 2½.

Similarly, your child may say 'No' if you ask her if she wants a biscuit, even though she wants one. Again, she simply thinks that she's using the correct word to answer a question – and if you say to her 'Do you want a biscuit, yes or no?' she is even more likely to say 'No' whether she wants one or not.

Don't worry too much about correcting her – she'll soon stop muddling her words as her speech improves. In fact, you can enjoy how charming her answers are to all sorts of questions such as 'Are you a girl or are you a boy?' – she'll say a boy. Your child will love this game and is too young to mind in the slightest that she is being gently teased – she'll just relish the attention and enjoy the conversation.

MILESTONES ☆☆☆

(All babies are different – you probably won't be able to tick everything on this list.)

☐ *Can open doors* – if the handle is within reach, she'll be able to work out how to open it.

☐ *Pushes furniture* – she'll have great fun moving chairs, small tables and other pieces of furniture that are not too heavy.

☐ *Can fit lids on boxes* – lots of children this age have the cognitive ability to understand that some things fit together, and also the dexterity to do it. As well as boxes with lids, you can give your child simple wooden jigsaws because she'll probably have a good go at fitting the pieces into the right spaces.

☐ *Doesn't like sharing* – your baby may have been happy enough to share a couple of months ago, but now she's probably very possessive about toys and food. This is a normal developmental stage and is part of her defining herself as separate and individual – she has become aware of 'self'. It will take another 6 months or more before she has a sense of anyone else in the world and their needs. In the meantime she will need adult supervision to be able to share.

☐ *Cross-dressing* – little boys will love hairclips, sparkly shoes and pretty dresses just as much as girls. Meanwhile your daughter may want to shave like Daddy and wear his tie. Children are naturally curious about just about anything, and have little idea about different genders before the age of about 3. So if your 2-year-old son insists on dressing up as a fairy, it's absolutely no indication of his final sexual orientation.

☐ *Brushes her own teeth* – some children are able to have a go at brushing their own teeth around now, although you need to help to ensure they do a thorough job. If your child hates having her teeth brushed, it's better that she does it herself than nothing at all, and as we've said before, she will probably become more cooperative after her second birthday.

☐ *Better at getting what she wants* – instead of crying or shouting for something, lots of toddlers are able to ask for a drink or a particular toy, and will pull at your clothes to get your attention so they can show you what they want you to notice.

WHEN TO WORRY

If your baby is still sleeping particularly badly at night and waking more than twice in the night three times a week, you might benefit from getting some professional help – you will no doubt be utterly exhausted. First your doctor will check that there are no problems causing your baby's broken sleeping pattern. Then you will be referred to a sleep counsellor who will support you in teaching your baby good sleeping habits.

SAFETY TIP OF THE MONTH ⓘ

Now that your toddler is getting bigger she will seem more robust and you'll probably be more boisterous with her when you play. Most parents have great fun swinging their toddlers around by their hands and arms – but this is actually quite dangerous. Although some people talk of dislocated shoulders, this won't actually happen. What's more likely is that your child ends up with a pulled elbow, especially if you swing her by just one arm, which puts even more strain on the joint – the forearm bone can slip out of the elbow joint. This can occur in the under-5s because the joint is not yet fully developed. If your child suffers a pulled elbow she will be in sudden pain and her arm will hang loosely. She'll need to go to hospital and her bone will have to be manipulated back into place. But once this is done, she'll make a quick recovery.

WHEN TO SEE THE DOCTOR ✚

Toddler diarrhoea

If your child does three or more loose poos a day and you see undigested food such as peas, carrot or sweetcorn, she probably has toddler diarrhoea. Your child will otherwise be well, and grow normally – symptoms usually begin shortly before the age of 2 and disappear between the ages of 3 and 6.

You only need to see a doctor if your child has a fever, isn't gaining weight or if she has blood or mucus in her stools. And of course, take her along to the doctor if you are in any way worried.

The cause of toddler diarrhoea is thought to be linked with the fact that the bowel of some young children doesn't absorb enough water. But as your toddler grows, her bowel will become more efficient and the problem should clear up.

There isn't a treatment for toddler diarrhoea, although it can sometimes help to cut back on the amount of squash and fruit juice your child drinks – the sugar in these drinks keeps water in the bowel, making poos watery.

It's also very common for toddlers to pick up viruses which cause gut infections and diarrhoea. Your child will seem obviously unwell and perhaps have a fever, vomiting and tummy pain. Ensure your toddler drinks plenty of fluids – it's fine to give squashes and fizzy drinks in this instance, because it's important to prevent dehydration. And see your doctor if the diarrhoea doesn't clear up within 48 hours, or if there is blood in the stools. Sometimes diarrhoea is caused by a bacterial infection which needs treating with antibiotics.

WHAT'S HAPPENING TO MUM AND DAD

Toddlers can drive even the most patient parents right to the edge – most small children seem to have an innate ability to push their parents' buttons and drive them crazy to get attention. Do be aware of the effect this can have on your relationship.

If you've had your buttons pushed you'll go into angry primate mode and will feel stressed and have less control over what you say and do. It's quite common for parents to yell at each other in these situations – better than yelling at a small child.

If this happens, try to step back and see the situation for what it is: you're both stressed because your toddler has been grizzling non-stop for 20 minutes because she wants the sweets she saw in the newsagent's. Now she's so frustrated that she's just taken her hat off and chucked it in a puddle, which means she'll get cold and probably cry even more. So you start blaming each other: 'Why didn't you pack a spare hat?' 'Why didn't you stop her chucking it in the puddle?' 'I didn't even want to come out in the first place,' and so on.

Make allowances for your partner in situations like this, and hope that he or she will make allowances for you, too. It often helps if you can take a moment to imagine the same situation but where your child is behaving like an angel. Then ask yourself, would you still be bickering? The answer will probably be no.

PLANNING AHEAD

If there is a family history of eye problems or a squint, then book your child in for an eye test. Go via your GP, who will arrange an appointment with a paediatric eye specialist – high street opticians aren't equipped to test such young children. It will take a month or so to get an appointment, but 2 years is an ideal age to be tested because your toddler will be old enough to cooperate during the test, but young enough for any eye problems to be easily rectified.

MONTH **22**

INTRODUCTION

Throughout this book we've sometimes referred to 'particularly lively' children, and more often than not this description can be applied to boys. As parents of four boys and two girls between us, we're convinced that boys and girls differ in their behaviour – little boys tend to be much livelier and more energetic than girls, who often seem to be naturally more sensible and mature.

This is partly due to brain development. In very young boys, only the left-hand side of the brain, which thinks analytically, tends to be used. However, girls use both the left-hand side and the creative right-hand side at the same time, because the neural pathway between the two sides is more efficient. This difference in brain development continues until the age of 5, when boys catch up. In the meantime, girls' brains are literally more mature, and this can explain why girls often develop language skills earlier, and why little boys are usually more impulsive, less able to communicate and often 'harder work' than girls.

The difference between boys and girls often seems more pronounced after the age of 2, although there are noticeable differences before then, of which you are no doubt aware.

If you're the parent of a little girl, it's helpful to be aware of these physiological differences because you will be more tolerant of boys – particularly when they're tearing around playgroup and come crashing into your daughter.

Parents of boys can take some consolation from the fact that their sometimes wayward toddler son isn't a reflection of their parenting skills. He actually has a more immature and impulsive brain than his female playmates.

Our big tip for parents with energetic boys – and this becomes more important as they get older – is to ensure your son gets plenty of exercise. Physical activity has a calming effect on all children and is crucial. But with lively boys, you'll actually see their behaviour deteriorate if they go too long without exercise.

So ideally take your son out twice a day, just as you would a big dog. If you kept a dog cooped up all day at home you wouldn't expect it to behave well, so why expect any more from your son? Give him the chance to run around outdoors, encourage him to walk as far as he can instead of going in the buggy, and take him swimming or to a soft play area – anything that will tire him out. And if the weather is too bad to go out, turn on the music and encourage him to jump, or get the cushions off your sofa so that he can have a climb. You'll see an instant improvement in his behaviour.

It goes without saying that all children are different, so plenty won't fit the boy/girl stereotype. It can be particularly difficult if your little girl is a bit of a tomboy – perhaps she is late to speak, impulsive, and plays boisterously with other children – hitting and biting from time to time. You don't even have the excuse, 'Oh, he's a boy' and you may wonder what on earth you've done 'wrong'. You've done nothing wrong at all. You've just got a lively, physically active daughter. Like all lively children she will benefit from lots of physical activity. And you may well find that she naturally calms down a bit from the age of around 2 to 2½ as her brain matures and she is less impulsive – likewise, boys may calm down a little at this stage.

SLEEP

Aim: uninterrupted night sleep 11–12 hours
To bed early – about 7 or 8 p.m.
One lunchtime nap (1½–2 hours)
A total of 13 hours' sleep

Lots of toddlers start to drag out bedtime around now as they realize that when you say goodnight, you won't be back until the morning. Also some of them have the verbal skills to 'negotiate'. So you may find that your child insists on an extra story, says she's thirsty, wants the covers tucked in a certain way, or has to have her teddies arranged in a particular order.

While you're aware that you are being 'played', you will also find yourself not wanting to upset your child just before lights out because this would result in a lengthy calming-down session.

For this reason, it's very easy for bedtime to become extended by 30 minutes or more. So it's worth being aware of the early signs of bedtime fussing, then you can decide how to deal with it.

Plenty of parents relish the final minutes before their child goes to sleep and think nothing of half an hour's fussing. But others get frustrated and want to get on with their evening.

Our advice is to watch the clock and don't let things run on longer than you're prepared to deal with every night. This may be a minute or an hour. But if you put a time boundary in place, things won't creep out of control.

Stopping the Bedtime Fussing

Do note that children in large families usually fuss less at bedtime simply because fussing doesn't work. Mum hasn't got time to pander to their every need. Of course Mum will do what she can to please her youngest child, bringing water and so on, but she won't spend more than a few minutes –

time soon runs out because her other children need her. If her youngest is still very upset once she's got the others into bed, Mum may well go back and try to sort her out. But more often than not, the toddler will have fallen asleep waiting.

While you can't replicate a large family if you don't have one, you can follow a few simple steps that will help stop the fussing getting out of hand.

Four Steps to Reducing Bedtime Fussing

1. Prepare – make sure you have water in the bedroom and any favourite teddies or soft toys. Try to anticipate anything else your toddler may ask for (within reason, of course) and try to have it to hand.

2. Try lavender – a few drops of lavender essential oil mixed into the bathwater can have a calming effect on your child and help her to get to sleep more easily. And the lovely smell will certainly make you feel calmer.

3. Set limits – for example, show your child the bedtime stories you are planning to read before you begin, and put any other books out of sight. Perhaps stick to a certain number every night.

4. Make the bedtime ritual predictable down to the last detail – for example, when you finish a story, close the book and put it back in the bookcase, or under your chair, and tell your toddler you are tidying the book away before bedtime. As she becomes dependent on this ritual she will be less likely to ask for more stories. Having a few rituals in place can help speed up bedtime, as long as you don't allow them to become more and more elaborate.

Dos and Don'ts

Do allow limited fussing – help your child with any 'arranging' (covers/soft toys and so on) – but if she continues to fuss, tell her, 'that's enough now,' then say goodnight in the usual way and leave the room. Your toddler will probably cry and get upset, so go back after about 5 minutes and you'll find that she is far more easily placated. You can repeat this pattern until she is happy. Just keep your return visits very short – a minute is long enough.

Don't get into bed with your toddler (assuming she's in a full-sized bed) – this can instantly calm the most unruly child and seems like a magical quick fix for getting your child to sleep. But lots of parents soon find themselves having to lie down for 30 minutes or more in their toddler's bed, then creep out once she's asleep. This is not only a pain, but it doesn't teach toddlers how to feel calm and sleepy on their own. And, just as it is important to teach your child good eating habits, it's also important to teach good sleeping habits.

Troubleshooting

I've heard that if you haven't got your child sleeping from 7 p.m. until 7 a.m. by now then it will be almost impossible

It's never too late to teach children to sleep well at night, although some parents seem to find it more difficult to teach toddlers than babies. But don't let this put you off – even with babies it takes time and patience. Whatever the age of your child, you have to put the time and energy in to teach them. This can often mean that you get less sleep yourself and become even more tired before things improve. But it will obviously be worth it in the end. Follow our sleep guide throughout this book, which basically says to minimize the 'help' you give your child getting to sleep until she is able to soothe herself.

FEEDING

If children help to prepare a meal they're more likely to eat it because they will be interested in the food and also they will understand how it is put together, so won't be so afraid of unfamiliar dishes.

We mentioned back in Month 17 how some children will suddenly become fussy about 'unidentifiable' foods – casseroles, or foods served with sauces. It is suddenly important that they recognize what they are eating.

Here are some suggestions for letting your toddler be involved in the kitchen – each idea involves preparing the food *before* it goes in the oven or on the hob, so nothing is hot. Do wash her hands before and afterwards, particularly if she may have touched any raw meat or fish, and make sure she doesn't touch her face or lick her fingers – have wipes to hand.

How Your Toddler Can 'Help' Prepare Meals

- Add handfuls of chopped carrots and other vegetables to a casserole.
- Stir in a tin of tomatoes, chopped onions and parsley to ready-prepared meatballs. A wooden spoon and a very large pan will help to minimize spills.
- Pick rosemary or other herbs, crunch them up and sprinkle them over a joint of lamb – you can also use dried rosemary.
- Roll baby potatoes in olive oil and herbs before putting them on a baking tray to be roasted.
- Sprinkle cheese onto a lasagne.
- Whisk up eggs for scrambled eggs or an omelette – you hold the hand whisk, your toddler turns the handle.

- Wrap up fish, for example salmon, in baking paper and foil to be baked.
- Brush milk onto pastry, apple or meat pies, to give them a sheen.

There are dozens of jobs that your toddler can help with. She only has to be involved for a couple of minutes – she'll probably get bored if it's much longer and the meal will take you twice as long to prepare.

If you can get into the habit of letting her see what goes on in the kitchen, she'll be more enthusiastic about food.

DEVELOPMENT AND PLAY

Talking

Lots of children are saying plenty of words by now, but it can take a few more months before you are really chattering with your toddler. In the meantime your child will be able to understand far more than she can say, so make a point of explaining to her what's going on. As you plonk her in the buggy and dash out, try to remember to tell your toddler where you are going, otherwise she won't know whether she's going to arrive at the swimming pool, the shops, the library or her nursery. If you have to dash off in a hurry, take a minute to explain to her where you are going, who's going to look after her and when you'll be back.

Your child may start to enjoy saying challenging words around now, such as 'dustbin lorry' or 'octopus' – of course she'll say them in her own way, with some adorable mistakes.

Some children call their parents by name around now, which can seem strange but is also quite amusing. This phase doesn't usually last long.

Swearing

The other thing that happens as children become more competent at speaking is that some of them swear. So if your toddler drops something she may exclaim, 'Oh, sh*t'. Resist the temptation to gasp in shock, laugh or indeed react in any way. Your child has no idea she has said anything wrong but is simply imitating what she's heard – for her it's just another sound she's copying.

If you make a fuss she'll realize that what she's said has impact and gets her noticed, making her more likely to say it again. One option is simply to ignore what she's said and carry on as if you haven't heard it. You could also 're-programme' her by giving her an alternative – 'Oh, sugar,' for example – and start saying this whenever you drop something. The crucial thing is that she doesn't hear any more swearing – there's nothing like hearing your child swear to break your own swearing habit. And if your child hasn't sworn yet, be warned, she probably will.

MILESTONES

(All babies are different – you probably won't be able to tick everything on this list.)

☐ *'Mine'* – most toddlers can say 'mine' by the time they're 2, and will no longer be fobbed off with a substitute toy. Developmentally it's normal for a toddler to roar 'My car'. This is because possessiveness is a natural developmental stage that happens once your child develops her sense of self (mentioned in Month 21). You may also notice that your toddler likes putting things in bags or loading up a toy pram or ride-on truck with favourite toys and objects, particularly if there are other children around, say at nursery or playgroup.

☐ *Plays alongside other toddlers* – she is still too young to play cooperatively, but will enjoy being with other children, watching what they are doing and possibly imitating them.

☐ *Washes hands* – at this age your child can probably climb onto a stool and wash her hands, and will be able to turn taps on (although she may forget to turn them off again). She will need help with soap.

☐ *Undresses* – around now your toddler will be able to pull off loose-fitting clothes such as elasticized trousers, t-shirts with wide necks and cardigans. She will still struggle with socks, tights and jumpers. Children generally learn to undress before they learn to get dressed.

☐ *Bolts in protest* – although your toddler doesn't wander off as much as she used to because her sense of danger is better developed, she is able to run quite fast and may rush off in protest if she becomes upset.

☐ *Less likely to fall over* – when she's running your toddler is now able to look down and avoid tripping over objects.

☐ *Makes demands* – as your child approaches 2, she'll start making more demands and you'll need to say 'No' more often. When you're tired you'll find yourself feeling worn down and it can sometimes be easier to say 'Yes' than 'No.' We all do this from time to time, and sometimes it's fine. But if you give in too often, your toddler will know that if she makes enough fuss she'll get her own way. Saying 'No' to a feisty toddler is a knack, and something that needs to be mastered. Our tip is to think about how you would say 'No' if you were sipping a scalding cup of coffee or a gin and tonic and your toddler wanted some. Your 'No' response would be calm, confident, absolutely decided and probably a bit amused, because the idea is so preposterous. There would be a lightness to your tone and yet your toddler would sense that there'd be no way you'd give in. We find this a more pleasant way to communicate than using the textbook firm, strident and commanding 'No', which can sometimes wobble and sound a bit indecisive unless you're a particularly firm, strident and commanding person. But however good your technique is, there will be days when your toddler is having none of it and has a tantrum because she can't have her own way. Deep breaths are the order of the day in these cases!

WHEN TO WORRY

If your toddler plays with toys only by banging, shaking or throwing them rather than using her imagination to push along a car, pour a kettle or attempt to get a cause-and-effect toy like a jack-in-the-box to work, it can indicate learning difficulties. If you're concerned, get her checked out.

SAFETY TIP OF THE MONTH ⓘ

Because your toddler is so much more dexterous now, it's worth ensuring that she can't escape out of the front door. Plenty of children this age have managed to climb up and open the front door, and some have successfully used keys which have been accidentally left in the lock. So get into the habit of not only double-locking doors, but hiding the keys, too. This is particularly important at night because small children often wake at dawn and can get into all sorts of mischief while parents are still asleep.

WHEN TO SEE THE DOCTOR ✚

Asthma

Before the age of 2, babies may suffer from a viral wheeze (see Month 12), which they will grow out of. Allergy-related asthma, however, can develop at any age from around now. This is when wheezing is triggered by an allergy – the small air tubes (*bronchi*) become inflamed and narrow, so you hear wheezing as your child breathes. She may also have breathing difficulties and a cough. And some children get a cough that didn't begin with a cold, goes on for weeks and is worse at night.

Genetics can play a part, making some children more susceptible if there is a family history of asthma, eczema or hay fever. Common asthma triggers include cats, dust, pollen and cigarette smoke.

It's essential to see your doctor if your child wheezes. If asthma is diagnosed, your child will be given Atrovent and/or Salbutamol to treat the breathing problems.

You can give these to your toddler using an asthma inhaler together with something called a spacer device – a big plastic container attached to a face mask that goes over your baby's mouth and nose (see illustration on page 104). This allows her to use an inhaler while she is still very young.

Your doctor will also advise on avoiding potential asthma triggers – so things like not staying in households with cats, replacing carpets with wooden floors to minimize dust and not letting your child play in grass in the summer, to reduce contact with pollen.

Always carry your child's inhalers with you, and don't be afraid to use them. It's easy to underestimate the seriousness of the condition, but children can and do die from an asthma attack, which is why it's essential to use the inhalers as prescribed. Don't be tempted to 'cut back' or to wean your child off her asthma medication – you won't be doing her any favours and will actually be putting her in danger.

WHAT'S HAPPENING TO MUM AND DAD

Parents with older children often look back wistfully as they remember packing their children off to bed at about 7 p.m. and having an entire evening to themselves. OK, older children aren't nearly as hard work during the day as toddlers, who need to be watched and monitored every waking minute. But do relish these long uninterrupted evenings – that wonderful feeling once the lights are out, your child is asleep and you can relax.

From about the age of 9, children start to stay up later, so you can look forward to squabbles over the television remote and lengthy negotiations about bedtimes. Toddlers, for all their flaws, thankfully can't tell the time.

PLANNING AHEAD

It's almost time to start thinking about planning your child's second birthday. She's old enough this year to enjoy having some toddler friends over for a party, while still young enough to be oblivious if this doesn't happen. So you've got the choice.

If you opt for a party, most children by about 2 are capable of sitting down for some birthday tea, but they won't be able to cope with any games more complicated than pass the parcel – and even this will require a lot of supervision.

If you decide to skip the party this year, your toddler will be delighted with a cake and a few presents. She's too young to have expectations.

As for presents, there's masses to choose from and you are bound to have some ideas, but here are a few suggestions. Toddlers at 2 can start to ride a tricycle and learn how to pedal, and some will start to manage a scooter or perhaps a wooden bicycle which has no pedals (designed to prepare children for a two-wheeler).

At age 2, children have the balance and coordination to enjoy tables and chairs scaled down to toddler size. And toys that help them mimic grown-ups are always popular, such as pretend toasters, irons, toolkits, plastic food and toy cooking equipment. Train sets and prams have been and always will be popular second birthday presents.

MONTH 23

INTRODUCTION

You've probably been told countless times by well-meaning friends and relatives that 'children grow up so quickly.' And now, as you approach your child's second birthday, you may start to see what they mean.

In the last 18 months your child has grown from a milk-guzzling baby who was barely crawling and tended to communicate by yelling or crying, into a busy toddler who can chatter away, run away, and argue away – usually about what she will or won't eat.

The journey from baby to toddlerhood is one of the most fascinating times of your child's life, and it's also one of the funniest. The fact that toddlers can make their parents laugh so much is an immense help when it comes to coping with the seemingly endless frustrations at times.

Your child will continue to push your patience to extremes, and to puzzle you with her behaviour for years to come. As you continue to try and fathom the mind of your toddler, try to console yourself with the fact that there aren't always answers, and that the solution for one child won't necessarily be the same for another.

One of the true wonders of children is that they baffle adults and will always do so. And as you muddle along in the confused journey of parenthood, have fun, because it's a magical time that will be over all too soon.

SLEEP

Aim: uninterrupted night sleep 11–12 hours
To bed early – about 7 or 8 p.m.
One lunchtime nap (1½–2 hours)
A total of 13 hours' sleep

Your toddler will continue to need a total of around 13 hours' sleep, including naps, well into her third year. If you find that she starts to cut back on her night-time sleep, you can shorten her afternoon nap to ensure that she is having at least 11 hours' sleep at night, ideally 12.

We mentioned back in Month 14 how your child's sleep pattern naturally matures with time; by now, most children will be sleeping more deeply. Even if your child is sleeping through the night, however, sleep continues to be an issue for most parents of small children and it's common to have problems with bedtime, night awakenings, and early mornings from time to time. Each of these problems has been covered in previous chapters, it's just a matter of referring back and doing a bit of 'retraining' whenever you run into difficulties.

We'd like to reassure you that it's very normal for small children to have sleep problems, and that you are certainly *not* alone. More importantly, whatever sleep problem your toddler throws at you, you will be able to sort out with a bit of planning and patience.

Troubleshooting

My toddler used to sleep until 7 a.m. but now wakes early, sometimes at 4.30 a.m.
The big question here is, is your child still tired or does she happen to need much less sleep than previously? We'd put bets on her still being tired – and if you're unconvinced, try giving her some extra help to get back to sleep such

as rocking, stroking her back or even giving her a bottle or breastmilk. Only do this as a one-off experiment to demonstrate to yourself that your child is still tired – you don't want bad habits to begin. Once you are convinced, you'll be in the right frame of mind to tackle the problem.

There are two things you can look at. First, her daytime naps. At this age, lots of children stop napping for so long, or even stop altogether during the day, and this can affect night sleep. But sometimes, reintroducing a longer daytime nap (of at least an hour) can help children sleep better at night and for longer in the mornings, because they aren't overtired and overwrought. Try doing something very active in the morning to ensure she is nice and tired for her lunchtime sleep, and this will hopefully have a knock-on effect at night. You can also try putting her down a little earlier for her nap – again, this can sometimes help reluctant nappers get off to sleep at night.

Another reason for early awakenings is teething – back teeth are often coming through around now, and this can take weeks. Because children don't sleep so deeply in the early hours as when they first go to bed, they are more likely to be roused by pain. Painkillers such as Calpol can of course help, but they wear off after about 4 hours.

There are two things you can try. One is to give your baby medicine, such as Calpol, at about 1 or 2 o'clock in the morning so that the effects will cover the small hours of the morning. This will probably mean setting your alarm for the middle of the night – worth it for a few nights, as you will find that once you break the pattern of the early awakenings, your toddler will no longer be troubled by pain because she will be used to sleeping through at this time. But you also have to consider how to give your toddler medicine without her becoming fully awake so that she can resettle quickly. Some children will manage this, but if yours doesn't there's no point in persevering.

Another option is to increase her bedtime dose by combining baby paracetamol (Calpol) with baby ibuprofen. These painkillers work in different ways, and combined will work in synergy to give a super-powerful but safe painkilling effect. The effects of ibuprofen last for between 6 and 8 hours, and even after this there will still be some effect. So hopefully this will help your toddler to sleep through for longer.

Don't worry about giving painkillers for teething night after night – baby ibuprofen will have no effect on her stomach lining, which is more resilient than an adult's because she is younger. And baby paracetamol won't damage her liver because toddlers metabolize this drug more efficiently than adults. Infant drugs are extremely safe, and most paediatricians happily give them to their own children very freely.

FEEDING

In Month 9 we set out guidelines so that you'd know what foods to feed your baby. These will remain the same once your baby turns 2, although the official guidelines say that you can start to offer her more fruits and vegetables – five portions a day instead of three.

If the thought of giving your child even more fruits and vegetables sends you into a bit of a spin, you're certainly not alone – lots of children become particularly fussy about food as they approach 2, and fruits and vegetables can be a problem, especially vegetables.

Thankfully, portion sizes for toddlers are much smaller than those for adults, so the task is less arduous than you may think. Here are some examples: a quarter of an apple, three strawberries, one small piece of broccoli, and five green beans each count as a toddler portion. Your aim at this stage is to get your child 'tasting' different fruits and vegetables rather than 'eating' them. Once she is familiar with a food, she will eat it in gradually bigger quantities.

Throughout this book we have emphasized how important it is to eat with your toddler, not to react if she doesn't eat something, and to try to stay relaxed. There's a final technique you can try which has proven results: offer a new food 10 times.

It's been shown that if you offer a particular food, say a green bean, to a child repeatedly, then after about 10 times there's a good chance she will actually eat it. So even if your child 'doesn't eat vegetables', keep giving them to her.

Banish Fussy Eating – Offer a Food 10 Times

- Tiny portions are OK. It's understandable you wouldn't give your child vegetables when you know they will only end up in the bin. But you need only offer her a tiny portion – one green bean, a single mushroom, a teaspoon of cabbage or sweetcorn, or a tiny bit of broccoli are all adequate. This keeps waste to a minimum.

- Don't go to any trouble. Save a little bit of the vegetables from your own dinner to give to your child the next day – you don't even have to warm them up, because if she's refusing to eat broccoli anyway there's no way she's going to know it's supposed to be served warm. You could also give her a little stick of raw carrot or pepper – again, this isn't much trouble and if you've not spent ages cooking something for your child, you'll be indifferent as to whether she eats it or not, helping to keep the whole process calm.

- Wait until she's hungry. Casually put some cucumber on her highchair tray just before you serve her main meal, when she'll be hungry. And there are no rules to say she can only have vegetables for lunch and dinner – try putting a slice of courgette in front of her while you mix her morning porridge.

- Lead by example. If you can, eat a little yourself of whatever vegetable you are giving your toddler. It's not easy to stomach cold courgette for breakfast, but this would certainly encourage your toddler to try some. And of course include her in family meals – even if it's just the two of you – then she can eat some of your vegetables if she wants.

- Persist. Your child may ignore the vegetables, perhaps she'll play with them or, once she's been presented with them often enough, she may even eat some. The key is to get into the habit of giving her vegetables two or three times a day. Then within a couple of months there's a very good chance that she will start to extend her vegetable repertoire. And it doesn't have to stop here – even with older children you can continue this pre-meal vegetable-nibbling habit by giving them the odd carrot or bean to munch on while you get their tea ready.

- As well as vegetables, this technique works with any foods your child 'doesn't like'.

DEVELOPMENT AND PLAY

Talking

Some children can say around 50 words by the time they are 2, and may be able to use three-word sentences – for example 'me want juice' or 'dog walk park'.

But if your child isn't saying many words and you're concerned, try writing down all the words she can say and adding to your list over a few days – it's often far more than you think. And it's normal for some words not to be very clear, because some speech sounds don't develop until later. Also, when your child first starts to put words together you may notice that she speaks less clearly – see 'When to Worry' for more on this.

At this age children's understanding will be surging ahead, and they can often understand two-step instructions and are able to memorize what they have been asked to do. For example, 'go into the bedroom and bring me the nappy.' By age 2, some children will have the memory and concentration to follow this request.

MILESTONES

(All babies are different – you probably won't be able to tick everything on this list.)

☐ *Tries pedalling a tricycle* – at around 2, toddlers are able to grasp the concept of pedalling and will have a go. A few will be successful.

☐ *Helps around the house* – your toddler will be delighted to help with everything from the laundry and unpacking the shopping to passing you things if you're with a new baby and you need a hand at bathtime or nappy time.

☐ *Walks upstairs* – she will walk up one step at a time and will need to put her hand against the wall or banisters for balance. She won't be able to walk downstairs yet unless you hold her hand.

☐ *Draws* – early signs of being able to do more than scribble, for example she may be able to copy a straight line, or do dots with a pencil or paintbrush.

☐ *Strips off* – most babies love being naked and having nappy-free time, but from around the age of 2 some toddlers will randomly want to strip off all their clothes and run around naked. If you are with family or close friends, you can allow your child to do this. Although most children don't have a concept of modesty until they are about 4, you may have to draw the line at stripping off in the supermarket. If you struggle to get your child to keep her clothes on, you could always have a dressing-up costume with you – she will probably be willing to put on a fairy outfit, or a little boy might be happy to wear a spacesuit.

☐ *Forward roll* – your toddler may be able to do a forward roll around now, and will love doing other simple gymnastic tricks and balances.

☐ *Kicks a ball well* – she probably won't fall over or miss so often these days.

☐ *Strongly right- or left-handed* – some children will use their favoured hand for most tasks.

☐ *Builds a tower of six blocks* – you'll have to show your toddler what to do, but she may have the manual dexterity to build quite a tall tower by now. You can also show her how to build bridges.

☐ *Still sucks her thumb* – if your toddler hasn't given up sucking her thumb yet, you may notice that her front teeth are starting to stick out. But don't worry too much, because most children naturally give up thumb-sucking by around school age. And their second teeth will grow through perfectly straight, so there's no need to attempt to get your child to stop sucking her thumb yet – there's plenty of time to do this in the future if she doesn't stop sucking her thumb spontaneously by about age 4 or 5. In the meantime, check to see how vigorously your toddler sucks her thumb. If she rests it gently in her mouth, she's less likely to have dental problems later on even if she continues to suck her thumb. But if she sucks vigorously, this is potentially more problematic.

☐ *Sees in colour* – your toddler can see in colour by now, and although her vision is almost as good as yours, she is still slightly longsighted, which means she's not as good at looking at close things. She'll have 20/20 vision at 3 years old. Don't worry if she has trouble learning her colours – this skill usually comes later, and it certainly isn't a sign at this age that she's colour blind. Colour-blindness is very rare unless there is a strong family history. It's also reassuring to note that if your toddler hasn't got a squint by this age, she'll probably never get one – but do get her checked out if her eyes ever point in slightly different directions. Even if your child's vision is perfect at the moment, however, this doesn't mean that her eyesight won't change throughout childhood. So continue to monitor her vision – eye tests for children are free.

☐ *Tries to make you laugh* – your toddler may have her first attempt at 'joke telling' around now, perhaps putting her trousers on her head or saying something like, 'I eat flies,' then roaring with laughter at the absurdity of this, and delighting in the amused response of her audience.

WHEN TO WORRY

Even if your child still isn't saying much, she should be making herself understood by pointing things out and getting what she wants in other ways. It's worth seeing your doctor if she's not doing this.

Also, if your child has a vocabulary of fewer than 20 words and is not yet joining two words together, or if you are in any way concerned, do see your doctor, who may refer your child to a speech therapist for assessment. If your child needs speech therapy she will no doubt have a wonderful time, because at this age speech therapy is play-based and lots of fun for small children.

If your toddler can't unscrew the top of a 3- to 5cm container, like a carton of milk, it may indicate trouble with her motor skills, so get her checked out if you are concerned. Of course she won't be able to unscrew tops that are tight or difficult to grip.

SAFETY TIP OF THE MONTH

Up until around now you have probably been watching your toddler almost all of the time. But as she approaches 2 you may find yourself not having to keep such a close eye on her – for example, you may suddenly feel comfortable with her playing upstairs while you're downstairs.

It's vital that you get window guards or locks if you haven't already done so. Climbing up and opening a window, then throwing things out would be a great game for a toddler, but obviously extremely dangerous. And this is just the sort of game she may well get up to as she spends more and more time on her own, unsupervised.

WHEN TO SEE THE DOCTOR ✚

Constipation

This is quite common as children approach potty-training age, because they develop enough muscle control to be able to withhold their poos if they choose to. Your child will be more likely to hold on if she is a little constipated, because she may find it painful going to the toilet if her poos are hard, dry and pellet-like. And, of course, if your toddler stops herself going to the toilet, it will exacerbate the problem – making her stools even harder and drier.

It's particularly important at this age to ensure that your child eats enough fibre, which is found in fruit, vegetables, beans, lentils, porridge, shredded wheat, Weetabix and brown bread. Increase fibre in your child's diet very gradually – doing this too quickly could give her wind, bloating, tummy ache and diarrhoea. One of the easiest ways to get toddlers to eat more fibre is to give them raisins, which are very sweet. Also, ensure that your child has plenty to drink, because dehydration can slow bowel movements.

If you notice that your child isn't pooing as often as usual, or that her poos are pellet-like, watch this pattern and take her to the doctor if there is no improvement after about 4 days. The doctor will feel her tummy and perhaps refer her for an X-ray to confirm diagnosis. Then your child may be given stool-softeners or mild laxatives on prescription.

Don't delay getting constipation seen to, because it can sometimes lead to anal fissures – small tears in the anus caused by forcing out hard poos – with a key symptom being some blood in the stools. This can be a very painful condition and will make your child more likely to withhold her poos.

WHAT'S HAPPENING TO MUM AND DAD

Throughout this book we've tried to make it clear that it's both common and very normal to argue more with your partner once you have a baby.

We haven't suggested relationship counselling in previous chapters, simply because when most new parents argue, it has little to do with their relationship and a lot to do with factors beyond their control, such as a lack of sleep. But deep down you will know if there are other issues at the root of your arguments rather than just irritability and tiredness, in which case it may be worth considering getting some professional help. If your partner isn't keen, you can always go on your own.

Thankfully, a lot of the domestic issues experienced by new parents seem to magically evaporate once their baby reaches about 2, and plenty of couples note that this is a real turning-point in their relationship. By now you've both had a couple of years to get your heads around becoming parents, and with better sleep and days no longer entirely planned around feeding routines, you'll be more relaxed and less strained together.

With any luck, you're both feeling increasingly confident and will be having more fun as a couple, both on your own and with your toddler.

Of course there may be other factors at play – if you've already had baby number two, you may have to wait a little longer before things settle down on the domestic front. But hang on in there, because it really does get better.

For extra support you could try visiting the website www.relate.org.uk – the site includes information on how babies can affect your relationship.

PLANNING AHEAD

Each month we've tried to give you helpful suggestions so that life with your toddler can be a little more organized – from when to buy a big bed to getting your application in for flexible working.

Being organized can certainly smooth the bumpy ride of parenting, but there will be times when life will become so impossibly disorganized you'll feel as though you are living in a washing machine and that everything is whirling around out of control.

Most parents experience this from time to time – all it takes is a bit of extra pressure, perhaps a big work deadline or a family event to plan, and life seems out of control. So you end up forgetting about a doctor's appointment, or you wait too long to get your child's feet remeasured – it happens. Don't be too hard on yourself; your guilt and anxiety will probably have a worse effect on your child than wearing a pair of too-tight shoes for a few weeks.

Anyway, if everything were mapped out and planned for your child to the last, tiniest detail, it would be a very rigid life. The muddling-along approach is not only easier to live by, it's actually better for your child, because you'll be so much more relaxed when life doesn't go to plan – and believe us, it won't.

As we leave you with your 2-year-old, it's pretty much impossible to advise on what to plan next. Just as each child is so very different, your relationship with your child and your journey together will be unique, too. This is what makes being a parent the most challenging and the most wonderful role there is.

MEAL PLANN

In this chapter we've provided lots of ideas for nutritious, easy-to-prepare meals for your baby, suitable for whichever weaning method you choose. For example, if you have chosen the baby-led weaning method, you may still find our puree section useful because you can use the purees as dips for your baby from when she is about 9 months old. And if you're giving your baby purees, you can offer her a selection from the finger foods from 6 months, as in combination weaning. Take your pick from our lists.

A BALANCED DIET

Once your baby reaches about 9 months old and is eating three meals daily, try to ensure that you give her the following each day:

- 3–4 servings of carbohydrates
- 3–4 servings of fruits and vegetables
- 2 servings of protein

Don't forget that snacks count, too – a banana would count as a fruit serving, a yoghurt as a protein serving.

Iron-rich Foods

Whether you're giving your baby purees or finger foods, try to include two iron-rich foods in her diet each day once she is eating three meals daily. Before this time she should have one to two iron-rich foods a day.

All of the following iron-rich foods can be pureed, or given as finger foods:

Meat

Slices of soft beef, lamb, pork or chicken – your baby can suck the juices from 6 months, although it will be a little longer before she is able to chew meat.

Fried lamb's or chicken liver – if you don't overcook it, this will be very soft and your baby may be able to gum bits off. You can also puree liver – it works well added to mashed potato.

You can puree any meat, then blend it with vegetables to keep it moist – you may need to add a little milk or water to stop it being too dry and difficult to swallow. Give this to your baby either as a puree, or rolled into balls and served as finger food. You can lightly fry these balls to help stick them together.

Eggs

Hard-boiled eggs – sliced for finger food from 6 months, or you can mash and add to meals.

Scrambled eggs – this can be spoon-fed to your baby from about 7 months, once she is able to swallow lumps, or you can let her pick up the lumps from around 9 months (she won't be able to pick the lumps up much before then because they are too small).

Lentils

You can microwave lentils in boiling water for 10 minutes with some chopped onion and a sprinkle of cumin powder to make a mild dhal. Add water to make the consistency more liquid for 6-month-old babies, and thicken up as your baby gets older.

You can fry lentil patties (spoonfuls of thick lentil paste rolled into balls and flattened out) to make finger food. Or your baby could dip naan bread (or ordinary bread) into the lentil mix.

Spinach

You can buy frozen cubes of finely-chopped spinach which you can microwave or boil in minutes. Your baby will be able to swallow chopped spinach from around 8 months. In the meantime you can put it in the blender to make a puree. Broccoli and spring greens are also good sources of iron.

Breakfast Cereals

Most are fortified with iron (check the packet), and you can give your baby mashed Weetabix from 6 months. Once your baby is 9 months old, she can have fun picking up dry cereal, which can make good finger-food snacks.

PUREES

One of the most effortless ways of making purees is, when you're cooking for the rest of the family, simply put a little of the dish aside to blend – you can either use a liquidizer or buy a cheap hand blender for about £10. You may need to add a little water or milk to make the consistency smoother.

You can blend whatever you happen to have cooked: pasta bolognaise, lasagne, roast dinners (leave out the gravy because of the high salt content), beef stir-fry (leave out soya and chilli sauce which are high in salt), salmon and pasta, home-made curry (ready-made sauces are very high in salt), casseroles – pretty much anything you happen to be eating.

Making meals from scratch avoids hidden salt – just put aside a portion for your baby before adding any salt to the rest of the family meal.

It's fine for your baby to have a little spice, just avoid ready-made sauces which can be very salty. And also check the food isn't so spicy that she burns her mouth or she will be put off a particular dish for a very long time.

You can also make up batches of purees from scratch – sweet potato, carrot and white fish poached in milk, minced beef and tomato, broccoli – the list is endless. Once the food is frozen, you can select three cubes from the freezer to be combined into a meal.

As well as freezing foods individually, you can also cook up meals especially for your baby, to freeze in batches – for example pureed chicken with courgettes, mashed sweet potato and lime juice; or pureed beef, carrot and potato.

Freezing and Defrosting Purees

You can freeze purees in ice cube trays, or you can buy special puree trays that have slightly bigger cubes. Put the prepared purees in the trays, pop the trays in labelled freezer bags, then, once cooled, put the trays in the freezer – putting them in while still warm may defrost other foods. Once they're frozen you can pop them out of the mould and store them in a sealed, labelled freezer bag, so that you can reuse the trays for other purees.

To defrost, microwave three cubes on full power for a minute, stir thoroughly, then microwave for a further 30 seconds. Purees should be heated all the way through to boiling – stir and allow at least 5 minutes' cooling time.

You can also boil frozen cubes in a saucepan, or take them out of the freezer and into the fridge the night before to be boiled in a saucepan the next day.

MASHES

Mashing is a quick way to prepare food for your baby and is less hassle than blending. The most obvious one to start with is mashed potato – add a little butter and plenty of milk to make it easy to swallow. You can also try mashed sweet potato.

Short-cuts

You don't have to peel and boil – simply put a whole potato or sweet potato in the microwave for 10 minutes, then scoop out with a spoon, before mashing.

Some fruit works well mashed – try strawberries, banana, peach, nectarine and melon. Try mixing some of these together and adding squeezed orange or lime juice for added vitamin C and a different taste.

You can also mash avocado and tofu, which you don't have to cook first.

FINGER FOODS

Even if you start your baby on purees rather than finger foods alone, you can offer finger food at each meal, as in combination weaning.

6 Months

When you begin at 6 months, cut the food into large batons or slices so that your baby can pick it up easily in her fists and gum it. Make sure everything is large enough for her to grasp, and don't overcook or it will be too mushy for your baby to pick up.

Our list begins with foods that are soft, dissolvable and easy to swallow, as well as foods that your baby will simply suck on.

Take your pick from the following:

- spear of cooked broccoli or cauliflower
- large cooked carrot or parsnip
- banana
- slice of toast, cut in half
- sticks of mild cheddar
- asparagus spear
- pear, peeled and cut into quarters
- slice of melon – wash the peel, because your baby is bound to suck it
- slice of peeled pineapple
- peach or nectarine, peeled and cut into quarters
- large strawberry, cut in half
- half a boiled potato, peeled
- oven chips
- pancake
- Yorkshire pudding
- white filleted fish – fry it to make it easier to pick up (check for bones, and avoid smoked fish as it is too salty)
- chunks of fresh tuna dipped in ground cumin and fried in olive oil for a few minutes (don't overcook or it will become dry and more difficult to eat)
- salmon fillet cut into large cubes, dipped in lemon juice and chopped herbs such as coriander, then fried in olive oil
- eggy bread – mix up an egg with a little milk then dip a slice of bread in it, fry one side, turn and fry the other side, then cut into wide strips
- meatballs, cut in half
- chunk of cooked steak, pork or chicken to suck

8 Months

At 8 months, your baby can move on to foods that require more dexterity. She may manage to pick up smaller pieces of food, and will also cope better with lumpier, less dissolvable food such as rice, which is more difficult to swallow.

Take your pick from the following:

- pasta shapes
- rice – choose sticky varieties, such as Thai, because it will be easier to pick up the clumps of rice
- satsuma – peel the skin off each segment (after your toddler is about a year old, you can simply cut segments in two to make it easier to eat)
- oranges – again, peel each segment (no need to peel segments after about a year, just cut up)
- green beans
- grated cheese
- grated raw apple
- chicken drumstick – remove the skin
- bread – because your baby can progress beyond toast, you could try making sandwiches

9 Months

By around 9 months, your baby's pincer grip will develop, enabling her to pick up even quite tiny pieces of food. She may even have the dexterity to cope with dips – dips are a great way to use up any purees you may have in your freezer. Your baby will also be better able to manage harder foods, and if she's teething will enjoy sucking at things like raw carrot sticks.

Take your pick from the following:

- meat cut into tiny pieces (as small as raisins)
- blueberries, cut in half
- grapes, cut in half
- raisins
- peas
- raw carrot batons
- raw apple slices, peeled

DIPS

These dips include ideas for nutritious meals, snacks and desserts for your baby:

- courgette batons with a pureed beef and potato dip
- unsalted chips with a carrot and lamb puree
- sticks of raw pepper with a pureed avocado, tomato, butter bean and garlic dip
- half a banana with a strawberry, raspberry and yoghurt puree
- sliced strawberry or melon dipped in yoghurt
- broccoli with a pea and bean puree
- cauliflower with a cheese sauce
- carrot batons with a lamb and potato puree
- courgette batons dipped into a pork, orange juice and sweet potato puree
- naan bread with lentil dhal (see iron-rich foods, page 238)
- bread sticks with hummus
- oven chips with a mushy pea and whitefish puree
- strips of fried lamb's liver with a mashed potato and mashed carrot dip

Do note that we have included some expensive ingredients such as asparagus, blueberries, tuna and salmon, but these are packed with nutrients and your baby will only want tiny amounts.

EATING WITH YOUR BABY – FROM DAY 1

The idea of eating together is very charming, but the reality is that your baby won't be eating much variety to begin with and will probably dine at strange times of the day.

With a bit of planning, though, it's still possible to share meals with your baby – her very first meal could theoretically be pureed roast beef, green beans and potato, together with a slightly larger slice of beef to suck as well as a bit of broccoli and a Yorkshire pudding. Of course she's unlikely to eat much of this, but will probably have fun playing with all of the new textures and shapes.

It's not always practical to have big family sit-down meals with your baby, but there are plenty of simpler ways to eat together. Here are some suggestions:

- Have breakfast together – you can both have Weetabix, porridge or other low-sugar, low-salt cereals.
- Share a banana – let your baby see you peel it, then you take the first bit and hand it to her to play with or eat.
- Tuck into a bowl of puree together – of course, you'll probably want to leave out the added breastmilk or formula! But you can give your baby her own spoon, then feed her and even let her feed you. It's a great way for you to increase your vegetable intake, although admittedly it will be messy.
- Cut up a pear, avocado or peach and eat it together – make sure your baby's slices don't have peel. And let her pick up her own slices, or she can hold the whole fruit and suck.
- Share some oven chips (unsalted).

A WORD ABOUT VEGETARIAN BABIES

If you are considering giving your baby a vegetarian diet, you can follow these guidelines to ensure she gets enough protein and iron.

First, you'll need to give your baby two good sources of protein every day – these include eggs, pulses, tofu, cheese and yoghurt.

Your baby can get her iron from the following (our list begins with the vegetarian foods that have the very highest iron content): kidney beans, mung beans, lentils, tofu, and dark green leafy vegetables such as spinach and broccoli.

Give your baby plenty of vitamin C (blueberries, strawberries, red pepper and citrus fruit) because this helps iron absorption.

RESOURCES

Argos

www.Argos.co.uk
For a hand blender

Bookstart

www.bookstart.org.uk
Free books for babies

Boots

www.boots.com
To buy a door stop

MMR Information

http://news.bbc.co.uk/1/hi/health/1808956.stm
The Meningitis Research Foundation
Free 24-hour helpline 080 8800 3344
www.meningitis.org.

Mothercare

www.mothercare.com
To buy furniture straps

NHS Direct

0845 4647
www.nhsdirect.nhs.uk

NHS Healthy Start

www.healthystart.nhs.uk
Children's vitamin drops

Relate

www.relate.org.uk
Relationship advice

Simone Cave

www.yourbabyandchild.com
Answers to the trickiest childcare questions

Stress Management Society

www.stress.org.uk
How to be a stress-free mum

Which?

www.which.co.uk
Car seat reviews

INDEX

Baby and Toddler Medical Conditions

www.yourbabyandchild.com

This is the website that answers the trickiest childcare questions. It guides you through the ups and downs of parenting and isn't afraid to tackle the subjects that no one else likes to talk about – so you'll never feel alone. Here are just a few of the questions covered on the site:

- I don't want to breastfeed, how do I stop my milk when my baby is born?

- I'm desperate to breastfeed my newborn but I don't have much milk, how do I make more?

- My baby won't stop crying, it's driving me insane and sometimes I hate her. Why am I so weird?

- We went to a birthday party and my child sat on my knee and wouldn't join in. What's the matter with her?

- My 6-year-old wets the bed every night – is he emotionally disturbed?

- At playgroup, my toddler behaves like a thug – hitting and biting other children and never sharing. What have I done wrong?